For L

May you always find your way home, even in the darkest night. I will be your light should you need one, you hope if you run out, and your safe and loving place to call home, when you are ready.

Forward

As we finished our first day together on the
beach, we stood hand in hand watching the
kids, both hers and mine, having fun in the
white sand and enjoying the warm gulf waters.
For my children, then 21, 14, and 10, it was
the first time they had seen the Gulf of
Mexico, or experienced a vacation like this.
And for hers, 19,17,14, and 11, they were just
happy to be there and finally beginning to
warm up a bit to mine as we had hope for. A
chance to merge the families and give them all
the opportunity to get to know each other.
We told the older kids to keep an eye on the
younger ones and we set off on a walk down
the beach at the water's edge. This was a trip
we had planned for a couple months. Our
relationship had taken off so fast. The
intensity of our love was like nothing we had
ever felt before or even heard of. We had both
mentioned over the short time we had been
together that this really felt like it was meant
to be. As if it was god given. It was scary,
how intense it was, but a good sort of scary.

As we walked we talked about the kids, and what we might do later that evening. We discussed how nice it was to be there, and how the Gulf water has this calming effect. We mentioned how if we ever got married, we both wanted it to be on the beach. We stopped for a minute and looked back, checking on the kids. I reached around her waist and pulled her close. I couldn't resist. After I kissed her, I just stared into her eyes. Such amazing eyes. It was, in a way as if I was looking into not only her soul, but mine as well. It was mesmerizing. And she felt it to. We turned and began walking again, and after only a few steps, I looked down to find a shell. A few more steps, I found something else.

I saw a glimpse of something silver in the sand at the water's edge. Waves gently rolling over it. I stopped and bent down and I could see it was a ring, buried in the sand. I picked it up and it was in the shape of a woman's crown.
This was no trinket. It appeared to be very old, and god knows how long it had been in the water before it washed up on shore.

We cleaned it off in the water, and it shined as if it were brand new. Sterling silver with small diamonds outlining the crown itself. It was beautiful, and we both just sort of looked at each other and knew this was a sign. This love was in fact much, much deeper and spiritual than any other. I gave it to her to try on and of course it fit perfectly.

When we returned to the house we were staying at we showed the kids what we had found. And even they seemed a bit in awe. None said anything but it just seemed too obvious that someone out there was sending her and I, a message.

This was I think the first time we both recognized the sign given, not to one of us, but to both of us. And to this day, even in separation, I'm told she still wears that crown every day. She knows the meaning it represents.

As I sit here attempting to write this, I'm struck with a bit of anxiety. Sort of like...What in the world are you doing? I have no idea where to start. So I guess as I once heard the Good witch tell Dorothy...It's always best to start at the beginning. So here we go..

My name is Patrick. I contemplated changing it for the purposes of protecting my identity along with the others in this book, but somehow that felt wrong. So with that said, readers should know that everything in this book is 100 percent true and authentic to the best of my recollection. Let's hope I don't get sued.

Anyway, I decided to attempt to write this, because I felt led to. There's no other explanation I can give. Writing is not my forte, but there is so much to say. I have read dozens of books and countless articles talking about the subject of soulmates and twin flames. Some of it was very beneficial to me and helping me to understand what it is I was dealing with. Other stuff was ridiculously far-fetched and clearly the authors had never experienced what real twin flame connection is, and I can only assume they saw an opportunity to prey on innocent people who desperately need advice and guidance.

The things that for me were the most beneficial, were the stories of personal journeys, and experiences. The ones written by ordinary people that we can relate to. The Authors that have been through the separation stages, and the dark nights. Those that have been the runner, or the chaser, and can help guide us through it with their own experiences. These books, if nothing else provide a degree of reassurance that we are not in fact losing our minds or sanity. And, well, I anyway, found comfort in knowing I wasn't alone. That reading someone else's experiences that so closely mirrored my own in a way proved to me that it was in fact real. And book after book story after story everything for the most part was the same. That's not a coincidence.

So I was on the jobsite today, and I was thinking about my twin flame. And how only days before the typing of this book, she got it. You know, that light bulb, AH HA, moment. When everything comes into focus and made sense. She is the runner. And She now Knows it. I had been trying to tell her and send her subtle hints that this was what was going on but she wasn't ready to hear it. So I sent her a couple of books on the subject several months ago. Only now did she decide to open one up and the first thing she saw was a paragraph about how the runner acts, and reacts to the chaser. How terrible the runner can treat the chaser and the reasons they do this.

The moment she saw this, she texted me a picture of the page she was reading. The message said,

"This is us! I am the runner! OMG!"

My response was simple.

"Yes, I know."

But the words on that page resonated so profoundly in her at that moment she felt excitement, and an instant feeling of hope and energy and wanting to know more. Even though for 2 yrs. I had spoken the exact words to her that she read on that page. Divine Timing at its purest. More on that later.

As I was thinking about this situation with my twin, it struck me that I should document our journey. At least from my perspective, as I can't speak for her. But I know how other authors stories helped me along the way, and now have helped her awaken. So maybe our story can help someone else struggling to understand, or give a little comfort in some way. I am not a writer. Please understand. I don't claim to have impeccable grammatical skills. Please just bear with me through the mistakes. i also do not in any way claim to be an expert in the field of twin flames or any other metaphysical field. I know there are some who will read our story and try to pic it apart. Because that's just what some people feel the need to do I guess. I don't care. If there's one point I'd like to get across with this is that even though you may read something and say WOW, that's exactly what happened to me...Please remember always, Every twin flames experience is different. A lot will be so spot on it shakes you to the core how closely it matches your own experience. But even if there's differences, it doesn't make any of it wrong. Your journey is as unique as you and your twin are. Your soul's lessons are not the same as mine or anyone else's. So please use this book as reference if necessary. Inspiration if it touches you. But most of all I want it to give a little hope. I know I needed it. And one more story from a new perspective might be a good thing.

I am writing this as it happened. Or should I say, is happening, since my twin has only recently been awakened. And as I said, I am not an author, I am a project manager for large infrastructure projects. So I think maybe the best way to attack this project is to simply tell the story of us first. I will tell it as I remember it, as well as attempt to tell it from what I know of my twins' perspective based on what she has shared with me over the years. After the story portion is complete, I will begin part 2. Where I will explain the synchronicities that occurred without our knowledge. As well as show the evolution from the "Bubble Love" phase as some like to call it, to the Runner, and Chaser roles. And how those rolls can switch. I will also give you our perspective on things such as, your spirit guides, and how they communicate. And signs, and symbols, that are put in front of you.

I hope this book is written well enough to give a clear view of what the Twin Flame experience is for us. And I hope I can explain it in basic words that all can relate to. So here we go... Wish me luck!

Chapter 1

As I sit here staring at the screen wondering where to start, so many thoughts flow through my mind. So I decided that maybe the best way to tell this story is to first introduce you to the Twins. Explain a bit about who we are as people, and hopefully that will give you a better vision of the story as we move forward.

Patrick

My name is Patrick. At the time of this writing I am 45 years old. I was born into a family of very modest means. I have 3 brothers, 2 older and one younger. My parents worked hard as I remember it. We never had a lot, but we always had enough. And they were the sort of parents that never used the words...I love you. But you always knew they did. Growing up, my brothers and I all played sports, and all of us excelled at all of them. Football, baseball, basketball, even bowling. There is a little over 2 years separating each of us. So the competitive spirit was strong in our family. And of course we all had our skirmishes, amongst each other, but when it came to an outsider trying to mess with one of us, they, soon found out there's 4 brothers and we protected our own. As I got older I became more of a loner. I had friends of course, but looking back on it, I should have had more, given the circumstances. I was the Quarterback of the local football little league team that never lost. That started at the age of 8 and never ended really, until high school graduation. On the field I was a general. I studied my playbook harder than any subject in the class room. I could read a defense, long before I ever read a book. And as I said, we never lost. In a town that loved Football. In a time when there was no other sport for boys.

Soccer hadn't become what it is today. I can only compare the atmosphere back then as what you'd see on television in the Friday night lights stories.

But off the field I was shy. I had my core group of friends, mostly guys from the team. But never felt as if I was any better than anyone else. I rarely had a girlfriend back then because I was so scared of being turned down that I just never could muster up the nerve to ask a girl out. And being the Quarterback of a team that was in the Newspapers every week, and even on the Television, I really always wondered if any of those girls really liked me, or just want to be seen with me.

To put it simply, I wasn't your typical high school, rule the school jock. I never realized or thought I could have been that. And looking back I am glad I wasn't. My eyes were open even then to what was going on around me. Both good and bad.

After High school both my brothers went off to the military. One to the Marines, and one to the air force. Unfortunately both were casualties of the Massive military cutbacks after the first gulf war came to a close.

I was not about to take that route. While military service was perfect choice for both my older brothers, it was not for me. I didn't even think about going to college until I received a few letters of interest, because of my days playing quarterback. That's when I realized I had options. I didn't have to just go to work in a factory after school. So I became the first in my family. Extended as well, to ever attend college.

I went to a small 2 year school, and graduated early. Of course back then I had big, big plans. I was going to make a million quick, and retire early. As we all know, that's really not how life works. And I was in for a rude awakening.

For the next several years I did what most people do. Try and find my way in this world. I was independent from the time I graduated college. On my own.

When I decided to go into business myself as a contractor, my father laughed at me. Told me I was wrong, told me I couldn't do it. Ironic, because he along with working a full time job, had a successful landscaping business as well.

In one years' time, my father was no longer laughing. In fact he was hinting around at merging his business with mine. A thing that never happened.

I got married at 23, and inherited a 4 year old who I adored. She was my wife's child who was born when she was 17. I loved that girl so much. A thing I would have never thought possible. But the natural instincts it takes to be a great dad just flowed. I truly viewed and still view her as my own. Time went on and business was hard. My wife at the time worked hard as well, basically being the financial stability of the family with her job, while I struggled most of the time with the ever changing market and demand of my business. Along the way, my son was born. And a few years later, my daughter was born. But things with my Then wife were not and had not been good for a long time. Though I would never have left my family or divorced my wife on my own, I prayed that god would intervene because I knew it wasn't right. And one day. God intervened.

She left me. There's lots of excuses, and reasons but the truth of it was, we got married young, and grew into different people. We grew apart. But there was one point after she told me she was moving out, she was sitting at the kitchen table, looking through the for rent ads in the newspaper. I looked at her, just knew, somehow I just felt, all I have to do is ask her not to go and she won't. I knew I only needed to say the words, Please stay. And she would. All would have been alright. But as I looked at her and knew this, I can say at the time I wanted to. I couldn't bare not having the kids with me. But the words wouldn't come out of my mouth. Literally. I couldn't speak. It was as if god took my voice to prevent that from happening. And she was gone.

A year later, Bankruptcy had come and gone. The house had been lost. And I was renting a little house closer to town. The divorce was well underway, and one night I received a call from her saying..."come get her, she isn't living here anymore."

I began to question her and what was happening and why and all of that, and as before, my voice was taken. I just stopped and told her to get my daughter ready I was on my way.

My ex-wife had had an argument with my then 14 yr. old step daughter. And it culminated with her mother throwing her out of her house.

I picked her up, and you could tell she was scared. All I told her was, it's a new start. We will figure it out together as we go. And that's just what we did.

I told my lawyer what had happened and that I couldn't understand how a mother could pick and choose what child she wanted and what child she didn't. And I couldn't live with myself if I didn't try to get the other 2 kids as well.

My lawyer laughed at me. Literally laughed. Told me I was wasting my time and money even trying because judges don't give custody to the father. I insisted on trying anyway.

I told my father what happened, and that I was going to try to get the other two back as well, and he said the same thing, Wasting my time, blah blah.

About 6 months later, wouldn't you know it? The judge awarded primary custody of all 3 to me. And since that day, I'm proud to say I set the example that Fathers can be more than weekend dads. All you have to do is try.

Several people I know have accomplished the same thing because I showed them the way.

As the time passed, money got tight. I had to move out of the little house because it wasn't big enough. So we found a trailer in town, that wasn't the best. But it was affordable. And the kids didn't care how nice it was or wasn't, they were happy that they were together. And that the town playground was right out back. But as the years went on, the trailer was run down. The land lord didn't do any up keep and there were nights when the heat would go out, and I'd be up trying to keep the house warm with space heaters and the electric oven. The roof leaked in about 5 different places and the front door wouldn't close all the way because the ice buildup under the threshold. Things were going from bad to worse.

Socially, I am a one woman man. I really only want long term relationships. But in the years now since my divorce, I had only really dated one woman. And she lived in South Carolina. Something that couldn't be overcome, and as you might expect, I found out one day she was cheating on me the entire time. But to my surprise, while I admit it did not feel good to find this out, but it only took about a week to get over. I just knew it wasn't right. And that there was something or someone else out there waiting to be found. So as the time passed I turned to the internet. Yep. Internet dating sites. And what I found was it was easy. I was meeting people every weekend. The problem was to the outside world, I was viewed as a "Player" because I was seen with so many different woman. The truth of the matter was, I was looking for "the one". I just had this feeling that being on this site was where I needed to be.

Ok, I will stop this section about myself there. And pick it up later, after I introduce you to my Twin. I hope this gives you an ever so slight look at who I was before I met her.

Chapter 2

Louise

Her name is Louise. At the time of this writing she is 47 years old. She too comes from a very modest family, about 50 miles south of where I grew up. And in a different state. She too has 3 siblings, 2 older and one younger, same as I do. Older sister, older brother, and one younger brother.

While I wrote in the previous chapter about how my family never had much, but we always had enough, Louise's family life was a bit different. Her father worked hard but the money wasn't always there. It would be wrong of me to say who's to blame for that, Mom or Dad, but the point is, she was left to fend for herself most often, and from a much too early age.

She tried to be involved in sports. She ran track or cross country, joined the cheerleading team. But was left on her own for the things that many take for granted. Like, a ride home from practice. The shoes she needed, etc. She would work a part time job when she could, to buy things for herself so she didn't have to ask her parents. And this also afforded her the opportunity to be out of the house as much as possible. Her mother had an un healthy favoritism for her younger brother, and her older siblings were already out of the house. Her father was not around much because he was always working to support the family. She was on her own more and more, and soon figured out that her parents really weren't paying any attention to her or what she did at all. She wouldn't just jump out the window and sneak off. She would just walk out the front door at any time of night at the age of 14 and no one said a word. It wasn't long after she found a boyfriend. At the age of 14, she was now with a man that was 18. Something that in this day and age would never be acceptable, and in fact is illegal. And as a father of 2 daughters, it made my stomach turn every time I heard Louise tell people about this phase of her life. Knowing that there's only one reason an 18 year old man, would want a 14 year old girl. But in fairness, she was, in my opinion, looking for the family connection, someone to care about her. The things she wasn't getting at home. And she did what she felt she had to in order to get it. But if you ask her about it today, if she would allow her daughter to have done the same things she did, she will tell you no way in hell. She isn't her parents, she's a mother that cares. And would never allow it.

Louise grew to learn who she could and could not count on. She was very strong willed and knew from an early age that whatever she wanted out of life she was going to have to get it on her own. However in retrospect, I don't think now looking back she would have it any other way. It's those circumstances that brought the qualities she needed to the forefront. Not just smart, but clever. Not just tuff, but brave. Not just loyal, but Protective of the select few she trusted. She grew to be very mindful in a way that she always thought things through, never making an impulse decision, yet she was fearless once she put her mind to something. And still today, she's been known to get a wild hair once in a while and blow off steam.

As time went on, she had her share of relationships. From what I can tell, none were very good. None with the loving aspect attached to it. Eventually she left her home town and followed her then boyfriend to another town a couple hours away. There, she worked and payed the bills while her boyfriend and a few of his buddies enrolled at a small college, and took advantage of her work ethic. She saw this as a way to move on from her home town, what she would call...another step in life. And she did so because she didn't know anything else. She was loyal to those she felt were loyal to her. But then things changed. One day her boyfriend came home from class and was mad about something. An argument ensued, and before long, he had her by the throat threatening to kill her. She didn't think twice. The trust and loyalty were gone in an instant. You see, Louise always gave her all to everything. And that included trust. But the second you broke her trust, you were done. You would never regain it. She packed her stuff and left. She went back home to her mother and father for a few weeks and remembered why she had left in the first place.

She packed her suv, and drove south. She landed in Rock Hill South Carolina, with no idea where to go or what to do. No job, no friends, nothing. But for the first time in her life she was free and on her own. And she loved it.

Eventually she landed a job, and made a few friends. And she enjoyed her new freedom. She was doing things on her terms, nobody else's.

Eventually she came back to her home town to visit her family and it wasn't long after that that she moved back home. And not so long after that she was pregnant with the first of 3 children. The father was not someone I think she ever intended to settle down with or spend the rest of her life with, but he had a bit of security to him, and he was fun along with the fact that they were young. And so because of the pregnancy, she had a bit of a rushed wedding. And I believe she did her best to be a good wife and mother, and then another unexpected turn. The birth of baby number 2.

By this time she realized, she was basically on her own. Her husband worked out of town all week long and when he came home he was no help at all with the 2 young children. To the point that she couldn't even get her husband to watch the kids so she could go to the bathroom. Or take a bath. She would actually have the baby on her lap while sitting on the toilet. Or bring both kids into the bathroom and have them read there little books to her to occupy them while she took a bath. She had had enough.

She told her husband it was over and moved out of the bedroom into the spare room until she or he could find a new place to move into. They were civil, after all he left town for a week at a time. And she didn't want fighting around the kids. Then one day he came home and they both went out to a bar with mutual friends. As she tells it, she was extremely drunk when she returned, and went straight to her room. Her husband went to his.

A few weeks later she finds out she's pregnant and can't figure out how. She hadn't been with anyone or her husband since she moved to the spare room. She asked her husband and he smiled and said that night they went out and got drunk, she went to her room and he went to his. What she was just now finding out was, he came back to her room and had sex with her as she was passed out and in no way could say no. And now .... Yep, pregnant with child number 3.

After the birth of her daughter, it didn't take long, and she was out of that house and the divorce was on. After a while she met the man that would become husband number 2. A man who for whatever reason was court ordered not to drink. And because of this he was good natured, and in general treated her well. And to her, she was just happy he accepted her as a single mom with 3 kids. But none of this lasted. Eventually the court order was lifted, and he began drinking and the good nature turned to a full blown drunk. A man that would lie, cheat, ignore his new family, treat the kids badly, and repeatedly disappear for days on end with no word. But each time he would return with guilt gifts and cry and beg for another chance. And she would give him another chance. And things would be ok for a week and then strait back to lying cheating, disappearing, etc.

Somewhere along the lines he convinced her to marry him so they got married at the Justice of the peace. Even now she will tell you, she knew she should not marry him, but she did because she didn't want to break up her family again.

A few years go by and the treatment got worse, the disappearances got longer. She told me once he actually had sex with another girl on the back porch while she was upstairs sleeping. But through the years even though she knew how bad things were, her friends would try to persuade her to leave him, and she wouldn't. She stayed true. And then one day she finally had enough.

I'm not exactly sure what the final straw was. But I know she made up her mind and that was that. He stalked her, followed her, left threatening messages, to the point that she needed a restraining order, and the judge ordered her to be given a pistol permit for protection immediately. After about 2 years of going through the divorce proceedings and him refusing to sign the papers, he finally couldn't stop the inevitable. And the divorce was done.

She would try to date. But she just couldn't find anyone that felt right. Her now ex-husband would do his best to scare off any one he saw her with. Yes still stalking her. She finally decided to try the online dating sites. She thought maybe if she finds someone from out of town, he wouldn't be able to follow her so easily and scare off people. And lord knows she wasn't going to find anyone in that po-dunk town.

So she made a profile and posted it onto a dating site. And not a lot of luck was had.

I will stop there, and pick it up in the next chapter. Hopefully this gives you some insight into what made us who we are and the kind of people we became.

Chapter 3

In the winter of 2013, I had been on a well-known dating site for a while. I had met many people. Some good, mostly bad. I had been on several dates, and was growing tired of it. While the site technically was working as advertised, it wasn't bringing me any happiness, and it sure wasn't bringing me the type of woman I wanted to meet. To be honest, if you had asked me then what type of woman, I did want I don't think I could tell you. But something in me said keep trying. I can't for the life of me figure out why I listened to that so-called inner voice. I was a single dad with 2 kids at home. I lived in a run-down trailer that had a leaky roof and at times, no heat. I drove a second hand work truck with over 200,000 miles on it. In short, I didn't really have a lot to offer.
It was after thanksgiving, that I had decided, I had had enough of the online dating. At least for now. The holidays were here and I was resigned to the fact that I was going to be alone again this year. I went to work the next day, which is where I used the internet, and canceled my subscription. But even when you stop paying for the services, your profile is still there for everyone to see.

As luck would have it, well my luck anyway, after I canceled my subscription, I came across her profile. One picture, not much written in the "about me" section. And I didn't even know where the town she listed as living in was. But I am and always have believed that as the old saying goes, the eyes are the windows to the soul". And even though it was just one picture, her smile instantly made me smile. I mean she literally made my heart jump. And when I looked at her eyes in that picture, I knew she was the one. But her eyes were as if it was her looking into my soul, not the other way around. In short, I was speechless. I was breathless. And I was smiling and I didn't even understand why. I immediately went to send her a message, and realized I had just canceled my subscription and couldn't. But there was a wink button, to at least let the other person know you were interested. So I hit that. And decided to wait and see what happened. After all, a woman like that wouldn't be on here long and most likely wouldn't be wanting a guy like me.

The next day, I came in to work and there was nothing. No response. I kind of expected there wouldn't be, and I was thinking it was a good thing I waited instead of just blowing more money on a new subscription for nothing. But my fortune was about to change.

Around Lunch time, I got a notification that someone had winked at me. I went to the site to see who it was. And sure enough, it was Louise. I was so happy. And I felt like an idiot for being so happy about a woman on a dating site winking back at me. Sounded so stupid in my head. But there was something else inside me that said it wasn't stupid. This is what I had been waiting for. This is what that inner voice wanted me to wait for. So of course now I couldn't wait anymore. I pulled out the credit card and paid for subscription so I could at least try to contact her.

I still felt like a blithering idiot, I had been on plenty of dates from this site, sent loads of emails. Yet, this time I was scared to death. I so desperately want to just not screw this up before it even started. So after a lot of thought I just decided to say this.....
"Hi, I just spent 39.95 to send this message so I hope you get it"

Can you believe that! How stupid can I be? I didn't introduce myself; I didn't ask her anything nothing. Damn I was done for sure. But then, a while later, I received an email from the site saying that she had responded. I couldn't believe it. I went to the site and there it was. Her picture next to a little envelope. This was her response to my message...

"I just spent 39.95 to read it so I hope you're worth it"

I just smiled and laughed. And that was the first hint of the amazing chemistry between us. From that moment on, we were stuck together like glue. I never had a conversation with a stranger flow so easily and quickly. All afternoon we spent messaging on this site back and forth. I didn't want it to end, so I asked about maybe texting or calling after work. And we exchanged numbers. Later that evening we texted a little but then she told me it would be ok to call her at a certain time, because she was trying to keep this entire experience away from her 2 children at home until such a time as it worked. So I waited, and when the time was right, I called.

I have to tell you, I don't know if anyone out there can relate to this, but for me, a woman's voice can be a deal breaker, am I right? Well, I'm telling you when she answered that phone, and I heard her voice, I felt it deep in my soul. It was the sweetest most beautiful thing I ever heard in my life.

We talked for hours! Both of us in disbelief because neither was the sort to talk on the phone at all. How amazing it was to not only find that connection neither had ever felt before, but it was instant. Like we had known each other before. Or we were old friends who hadn't seen each other in a while. I couldn't put words to feeling. And this went on for a couple of days, until I finally asked her to lunch. I took a half of a day off from my job, and drove to a restaurant we agreed was about halfway between us. When I saw her get out of her car I smiled and was both nervous and calm at the same time, I can't really explain it. And we went into the restaurant and sat and ate and again, talked for hours, in fact the only reason we ended the date was because we both had to be home to get our children from school. I walked her to the car and hugged her, and as scared as I was, I kissed her before I left. Which is something I don't do. I left the restaurant smiling and excited I couldn't wait to see her again. And that's a feeling that I had never felt before. Little did I know before I would get the chance to see her again, I almost screwed it all up.

Ok. Now let's change gears here and see this from Louise's perspective.

Around November of 2013, Louise had decided to go on a popular dating site. Mostly because the last 2 years had been a strain on her with the divorce and all, and she had taken her time to be sure she was ready to date again. She had dated a few men from her area, but none worked out. Seems they were scared of her ex-husband, who was still stalking her and would run off anyone he felt she was interested in. But she wasn't quite ready to give up on finding her true love yet.
She made a profile and she included one picture. A picture she had had taken by a professional photographer, who was related to her. You see, the events of the past several years had worn her down badly. The emotional and verbal abuse she suffered through daily from her ex-husband was constant. And after her second failed marriage, she was left with very low self-esteem. The photo shoot was suggested as a way to show her how beautiful she really was, from someone else's point of view and hopefully give her a little confidence back.

So she posted her profile and waited to see what might come of it. And in true online style, when you are new and a beautiful woman, your inbox gets flooded with all sorts of crazies and even some women. It was a bit overwhelming for her. Especially since some of these messages were from some really nutty perverts. A lot of them were from people so far away she would never meet them anyway. But there were a few she tried to respond to. However, in the end they really all were just looking for a quick hook up. And as soon as they figured out they weren't going to get it from her, they just went silent.

This went on for a while, and to my knowledge she never actually met anyone from the site. And it was looking more and more like a waste of time and money. The holidays were here and she just had given up on the whole online experience. So she canceled her membership, and had intended to delete her entire profile from the site as well but for some reason got side tracked, so she told herself she would do that later that evening.

When the winded down for her and the kids were in bed she went back to delete her profile and noticed that she had received a wink. So she clicked on the link and my picture and profile popped up. As she read through the profile and checked the pictures out, she wasn't sure what to do. She hadn't had a very good experience on this site so far and she only turned her computer on in the first place, so she could delete her profile. So, as is Normal for Louise, she slept on it, and would figure it out in the morning.

But when morning came, she had no more clarity than the night before. Something told her this was the one. Her heart told her that. But her head told her to be careful. So she turned on her computer and looked at the profile one more time and couldn't get past the eyes in the picture. Something she couldn't put her finger on or pin point. But she decided to hit the wink button and wait to see what might come of it.

An hour or so later, she received a notification that she had been sent an email, so she opened it and there was a message from me.

"I just spent 39.95 to send this to you so I hope you get it"

She just smiled, got her credit card out and renewed her subscription so she could respond.

"I just paid 39.95 to read it so I hope you're worth it"

And from there it was like nothing she had ever experienced. The conversation was so easy, and it was as if we had known each other for years. We laughed, and joked, and talked about our kids, and work, and what we did for fun. It was so nice. They decided to get off the website and text instead. But it was as if we couldn't get enough of each other, like an addiction almost. It was almost unexplainable.

She had given him a time that would be ok to call, after the kids were in bed, and he did. And it felt like we were school kids again. Couldn't wait to hear from each other. And it was so uncharacteristic of her to talk on the phone at all, but those conversations would last for hours! And just flowed like the most natural thing in the world. After a day or two, she agreed to meet him at a restaurant for lunch.

When it was time to leave to meet Patrick, she was nervous. But in a good way, Doubt tried to creep in because of the previous experiences. But everything had been so wonderful so far she couldn't help but be excited. When she pulled in to the parking lot she looked back before getting out and she saw him standing near the entrance. So she exited the car and walked over to him and they went in. And from there the nervousness went away for them both. She was amazed at how fast she felt completely at ease, as they sat there talking for what seemed like hours. My god she thought once, we talk so much, I never knew 2 people could have that much to say.

When it was time to leave, neither wanted the lunch date to end, but both had lost track of time and had to return to be with their children after school.

As he walked her to the car, she had hoped he would kiss her. Wow. Where did that come from? She wasn't a teenager anymore. But the feelings were there. When he bent to kiss her she was relieved. Even if her heart was pounding a mile a minute.

As she drove home, she found herself smiling the whole way. Finally she found the one. But she was cautious, with her past luck, something would come along and ruin it. Maybe her ex-husband would scare him off. But Patrick didn't seem like the kind of man to run from anything.

She returned home and checked her messages, and there were more than a couple from her friend and business partner, Anxious to know how lunch went. Her business partner had seen her through the bad times with her ex-husband. She knew Louise was due for a break in life, and was genuinely happy and hopeful for her.

That afternoon she talked with her friend and told her how good she felt and how positive everything seemed between us. That night as Louise crawled into bed she wrote in her journal,

"I found him".

And the feeling she had hoped to have for a very long time enveloped her. She couldn't wait to see him again.

Chapter 4

As I drove home from Lunch with Louise, I couldn't help but smile. How could this be? She was absolutely stunning. She had her own business that was growing. She owned her own home. Her 2 kids at home were the same ages as mine. We had the same aspirations and goals in life. We had a very similar past. Hell, we were already finishing each other's sentences, after only a couple days. What in the world is going on?

But as I pulled into my driveway, I stared at the rundown trailer I lived in. It was then that I noticed the beat up truck I was in. Even the shoes I was wearing, old and worn work boots. That's when the doubts crept in. I was scared that she would take one look at how I lived, and realize I have nothing to offer her. And as these thoughts went through my head, it was a pain, and hurt. The realization (or so I thought), that I would never be good enough for this amazing woman. But I held on to that kiss. I held on to that smile, and that laugh. And put the thoughts out of my mind for now.

Later that evening, after my children had gone to their mothers for the weekend, I received a call from my oldest daughter. She had gone off the road and into a ditch. Luckily everything was alright, but she needed money to get it fixed and was in a panic over not being able to work without a car to get back and forth. I told her not to worry, we would figure something out.

I had a few bucks saved, not enough to speak of, but it was enough to help her get the car into a garage to get repaired. So there, another crisis averted. It took a couple days but we got it done. And the whole time I was thinking about Louise. Ever since I met her I just couldn't stop thinking of her.

I wanted so badly to ask her out on a second date, but I was ashamed to admit, that I couldn't. I was broke after spending all I had on helping my daughter. In my mind I couldn't expect her to understand. And rather than just tell her the truth, I avoided having to tell her anything. I ghosted her. It was my ego and embarrassment that were to blame. And for as strong and honest as I always prided myself to be, I was weak when it came to Louise. Something I had never experienced before and keep in mind, it has only been a matter of days, not months or years.

All while Louise waited patiently by her phone hoping I would call. She couldn't for the life of her understand why I wouldn't. We had had such a wonderful time together, the connection was undeniable. Or was it. She began to think maybe it was all in her head. Maybe it was just her that felt it, and I was just being nice. Or maybe she had said something to offend me. Maybe I didn't find her attractive. All things that went through her mind while she sat there as a week went by with no contact at all from me.

Never once had she left my mind. In fact, the feelings I felt for her were only getting stronger. And I couldn't bare it anymore. I had to hear her voice. I had to make things right. But I just couldn't. No matter how much I wanted to see her again, I was so embarrassed. And to make matters worse, the heat went out in the trailer again. So everything I felt for this amazing woman would have to wait. It was December and there was no heat in my home, and I was broke from handling another crisis, the previous week.

It was a Saturday, a little over a week after our lunch date. I was sitting on my couch in the afternoon, keeping the place warm with space heaters, and the oven, waiting for the landlord to show up and fix the furnace. I looked down at my phone as the light went off. Louise was texting me.

My heart jumped, just at the site of her name. But I dreaded reading the message. It wouldn't be good. But I would let her be mad at me. After all she had every right to be. I would let her say what she needed to and she would be done with me. And maybe this wondrous, amazing, all-encompassing feeling would go away and I wouldn't have to feel embarrassed or ashamed. Or shed never have to know I wasn't good enough.

I picked up my phone and read the message.

"I get that you aren't interested, I just want to know why"

I responded,

"What do you mean?"

Of course I was interested. I knew exactly why she felt otherwise though.

"Everything was wonderful, going great, I thought anyway, and then out of nowhere you disappear. I just want to know why men do this to me"

It tore at my heart to have to have this conversation with her. As crazy as it sounds, I had only known Louise for a total of 10 days. And the last 7 we hadn't spoken. So in the course of 3 days, and one lunch, I can tell you, I was head over heels in love with this woman. I'm not sure I realized it then, logic tried to take over and explain everything in my mind. But my heart and soul knew and wasn't going to let me out of this without a fight.

"I can't speak for all the other people, but for me, I just been busy"

As pathetic as it was, that was my reply. And it was a lie. And she knew it. But she immediately thought "busy" actually meant, I was dating someone else. This was not even close to the truth. But a lie is a lie. And it's my fault she felt this way.

She finally replied with a message I'll never forget.

"Ok, well, thanks for clearing that up, I'm done with dating, if I want the company of a man, I'll just resort to random acts of kindness".

As soon as I read this I was angry. Not at her but at myself. I had made her feel this way all because of pride and ego? I was panicked. No way Louise was going to do the "random acts of kindness" she was way too good to feel that that was the best she could do. I couldn't take the pain and the hurt and the guilt of what was happening here. I didn't understand any of it. But I had to stop this. I immediately picked up the phone and called her. No way was I going to say what I had to say over text. No way was I going to take the chance that she might not think I was telling the truth, and honestly I was surprised she answered. When she did I felt a lump in my throat. One of guilt, regret, and also joy and happiness, just to hear her voice again. She answered with hello, and I immediately went into my explanation, before I lost my nerve. I went on to explain about the doubts that crept into my mind on the way home. How I never in a million years expected to ever find a connection like this, one that neither of us can explain. I told her about my daughters' car and the money I spent. And how I want so bad to see her again, but was too embarrassed to tell her why I couldn't. And I then went on to tell her about the heat going out in my trailer, and having to try to stay warm with space heaters. And I was waiting as we speak for the landlord to fix the furnace.

Talk about a humbling experience. On the one hand, I wanted to cry because I was in a lose- lose situation. If I didn't come clean this woman I already loved was going to go to give up on hope. If I did come clean, I was going to lose her because of my circumstances, AND be embarrassed in the process.

But I spilled my guts to this woman and when I was done I told her, regardless of whether she ever wanted to see me again after this or not, don't ever say you're going to do the random acts of kindness. I told her she is way too good for that or to even think that way. And the only reason I picked up the phone and embarrassed myself was so she would know the truth and not give up on herself. Now I was at her mercy.

Other than hello, she hadn't spoken a word. I just started talking and talking probably too fast, so as not to lose my nerve, but the whole time she remained silent. And now the first thing she said was

"Why didn't you just tell me? I have money, and we didn't need to go out and spend money, we could have had a great time just sitting and talking"

I wasn't prepared for this response. Her voice was loving, understanding, and eager to help in any way she could. I was prepared for the worst. Yelling at me, calling me every name in the book, (which I deserved) and eventually a hang up after telling me she never wanted to see me again. But this isn't what happened. All my life experiences had taught me that when the times get tough, the woman bails. And here we were, only days into this and this woman isn't running. I was. She wasn't ashamed of me, she felt the same as I did. Neither of us could understand why our chemistry was so strong. But it was clear to both of us that it wasn't normal.

She was relieved that in fact it wasn't that I was seeing another woman at all. And she never doubted my explanation because she could tell it was a difficult thing to have told her that truth. She knew that I was in effect, sacrificing my own pride and ego, to save her from a bad decision. And that is an act of love that most that have been in relationships for years don't do or recognize.

For, me... What a lesson in Humility. I have always been one to tell the truth, no matter the consequences. But I had never experienced a situation like this. The instant love, and devotion. The strength of the connection I've never had in the past, not even with my ex-wife. By humbling myself in the way I did, and giving Louise what she needed in that moment, only made me love her more. And she felt the same way about me.

We talked for most of the day and into the evening. I felt a peace in me that had been missing for so long. Maybe everything would be ok. Neither of us could quite put into words what was happening, but we knew something was. The next evening we decided to meet for a drink at the same place we had lunch. Kind of a try again type thing. We met at the restaurant as before and sat at the bar. As with every other conversation we had, it just flowed so natural and easy. And this time it was nothing but magnetism. We were drawn to each other so strong. I couldn't wait to kiss her again. In fact I don't think I did wait, I kissed her right there at the bar. It wasn't a sexual tension per se but just a feeling of, I can't get close enough to you. Of course the sexual attraction was there for us both, but in our minds it felt as if this wasn't just our second date, we were so comfortable together

it might as well have been or 10th date.
After we had a drink or two, we made our way
to the parking lot. It was dark outside so I
walked her to her car. Somehow, I don't
actually remember what was said, or how it
happened, but we ended up in the back seat
of her car. I only mention this, because I had
never done that before. Been on a date and
got in the back seat with her before. Never in
my life. So to say it was unusual would be an
understatement. But as I said before, we just
couldn't be close enough, couldn't get close
enough. But I'm happy to say we found the
control button, and didn't take it as far as it
very easily could have. We both felt that our
first time together was too special to be in the
back seat of a car. So reluctantly, we stopped
and eventually I found my way back to my
truck and we said our goodbyes.

But this time I wasn't letting anything get in
our way. In fact I called her when I got home,
to tell her how much I enjoyed being with her.
And how beautiful she looked tonight. I never
again would do anything to intentionally
jeopardize this beautiful thing that I could only
describe as god given.

From that night on there was no separating us. We still couldn't get enough of each other. Her kids eventually caught on that mom must have a new boyfriend, and tried hard to figure out who. She did her best to keep it from them. We had both agreed to keep this away from them until we knew it was for keeps. But kids are clever. And hers were especially sharp. They had seen their mother have to endure the verbal and emotional abuse by her ex-husband. They had seen the fear, and anger, and hopelessness in their mother for years. And even though they were young, her son was 13 and her daughter was 11, they could see that mom was happy now. She had a joy in her eyes, and a peace in her. It was fun keeping it from them. It became a game. My phone number would pop up on their television screen when I would call. And both of them would race to get the phone to answer before Louise could, so they could talk to me. And after a while, they figured out I would call at the same time every night, and go hide the phone so they could get it before mom. I sit here smiling as write this. I had more than a few conversations with them before we ever met. These memories are bitter sweet. Because I know that as of the time of writing this book, her son is 19, and her daughter is 17. And I haven't seen or spoken to either of them in over 2 yrs. And it breaks my heart.

But I digress.....

Chapter 5

As time moved on, I eventually met her 3 children and she met mine. I love kids. And I thoroughly enjoyed getting to know them. I worked hard to just be a positive influence for them, and to make sure they saw that I had nothing but love for their mother. At first, it was Louise's daughter, 11 at the time, who became very close with me. I think she just enjoyed the fact that I didn't treat her as a child. I spoke to her as an equal. And she loved the joking around we used to do. At that time, there father wasn't as involved as he could have been, and the kids had seen too much negative from the step-father. So I believe at the time they were just happy to see their mother smile again. And maybe soak in the positive attention from a male role model that loved having them around. It was all new to them as well.

But over time, I got to be the closest with her middle son. He was around most every time I was there. And through the years, we grew to be good friends if nothing else. And for that I have always been very proud.

The only real difficulty in our relationship over the first few months was that we could only see each other on the weekends. She lived in another town across the state line. And I lived here, with my kids. Neither could just up and move due to the rights of the noncustodial parents, and to be honest, we both understood that uprooting the kids would not be in there best interest. It was a discussion we had more than once, so we resigned ourselves to the fact that it was going to be about years before we could be married, or at least live together. It sucked, but we accepted it and moved forward.

But we wanted more and more time together. The initial feelings never subsided. As they do for most couples. You know, everything is awesome in the beginning. But then you get comfortable, and the feelings lose a bit of their strength. I guess it's called by some, dating the representative. It's only a matter of time before the real people show themselves. This never happened for Louise and I. In fact, even today, she will tell you, there isn't one day that went by that I didn't tell her how beautiful she was. Not once did she ever walk past me without me reaching out to touch her. Our feelings were so strong and building. Time was our only obstacle.

In April of the same year, 4 month into this journey, we decided to take a weeklong vacation in Florida. And we also decided to take all the kids with us. We planned for July, and we worked together. The kids were excited, and so were we. We spent countless hours talking about this and that, and the details of the trip. We knew it was going to be a bit tough for the two of us to get quality time while there, but we really were hoping that the kids would have a chance to bond and get to know each other a bit while there, and not just pair off and ignore each other. Doesn't sound like it would be that difficult to accomplish, but I'm telling you it was damn near impossible. With the exception of my oldest daughter, and Louise's former stepdaughter who was her children's sister. Those two bonded nearly instantly and even today keep in contact. But the others had a hard time finding common ground. In Hindsight, it's easy to see why. Louise's oldest son had brought his girlfriend with him. That alone meant he was preoccupied the entire time. And the girlfriend did her best to keep his attention all to herself. Louise's middle son, along with my son were both very shy around people they didn't know. Which made it difficult for either of them to break out of that shell. Her youngest, daughter was 11. And trying very hard to impress her older sister whom she didn't get to see very much. The only problem was the older sister was enjoying her time with my oldest, both in their 20s. Which made it difficult for an 11 year old to fit their plans. And as for my youngest, she was 10. And she was happy with anyone. Sometimes she'd spend time with her brother, others, she would be with her sister, or me. But she was very much the odd person out. Luckily her personality is such that she is always happy. Never complains, and is grateful for anything she has. And Looking back, I can see clear, that Louise was aware of My youngest and her not being paired so to speak, and made every effort to make sure she felt included and wanted. I never told her, but that meant the world to me to see.

The entire trip was awesome. At least from my perspective. We had our issues. The oldest son's girlfriend being there presented certain issues. The two older girls pairing off and enjoying having a few cocktails was unexpected. My son gets a bit...Socially awkward at that age. And had a bit of difficulty making new friends. But all in all, no matter the issues, we would do it again in a second. And it was a good learning experience for Louise and I. Both single parents of teens, the same age, but for the most part, 2 very different methods of parenting. But I think we handled it well. And the whole experience was just amazing at how well we worked together. It really was just …. Well not normal how smooth everything went. Even when we hit a road block, when we were on the same page it was like waving your hand and the problem was solved. I remember smiling, really for no reason. Just in amazement I guess, at how wonderful she was. And how my life had turned in just a few short months since id met her. I didn't know why. Or how it happened that we could so completely change each other's lives in such a short period of time. But it happened, and it was still happening. At this point we both knew that what we had was not normal, we knew it was a gift from god. But neither of us knew where it would take us, or how far. I guess we both began to wonder deep in our minds, when's the other shoe going to drop? The clock strike midnight? There became a point that I think we were both so afraid of the power of this love that we forgot to enjoy it. Forgot to be thankful for it. Kind of like winning millions in the lottery. Most people would think all the problems of life would be solved. But in some, it's so overwhelming that they become paranoid. And afraid of their good fortune.

That's kind of what was happening to us. Of course neither of us knew it yet. Or could see it. But the connection was growing so strong, but so was the fear of losing it.

Chapter 6

As time went on, the bond, if it was possible grew stronger and stronger. I could dedicate an entire novel to our love and the uniqueness of it. The wonderful feelings and things we did for one another. In fact we have joked even now, about how the movie, "The Notebook" so closely resembled our story. But I am only giving an overview of the relationship in effort to timeline our journey so to speak. As I write this, it is with a heavy heart. Bitter sweet, I guess. Reliving all the good. Owning all the bad. But as you read, keep in mind. Neither of us had ever even heard of the term "Twin Flame". We were completely ignorant to anything that was happening, and that we weren't actually crazy after all. We had had conversations over the years about being Soul Mates. But even that just didn't seem to be right. Somehow it's the strongest word we knew to use, but it just didn't feel powerful enough.

In time, Louise's business began almost too really take off. I mean, almost immediately after we met. She went from 50 to 100 sales a week, to 2000 to 3000 sales a week. Not dollars. That's individual sales. And exponentially more than that at certain times of the year.

I would stand back and try to help were and when I could. But to be honest, I was just in the way most of the time. I didn't tell her enough, but I was so proud of her. And all that she accomplished. She was and still is the most creative mind I've ever met. We used to spend days in the work shop just building whatever came to mind. And we loved every second of sharing something we both loved to do. She had a certain softness about her that no one ever got to see. But I did. I saw it in her eyes every time I looked into them. She had a playfulness that she never let out. But when she was with me, she did. And Looking back on it, I don't think she even realized it but, it was simply that she felt safe with me. To the world she would present this tough exterior that had been formed as a defense mechanism, because of her journey to this point. To most, it defined her. Louise, the beautiful, sexy, petite little woman, that didn't need anyone. She could do it all on her own and she could do it better than you. And if you pressed her on something you'd regret it. No one would ever see her cry, or get to close to her heart again. At least that was the exterior. That's what she portrayed. And in retrospect, probably what she believed. She never saw this coming. Never in a million years did she believe that the fairy tale kind of love story was in the cards for her. But now here it was and on one level, she didn't even know it was happening, but on another she knew, and it scared her to death.

We used to talk about our walls we put up. Everyone in life has walls. Certain barriers put up around certain aspects of our lives to protect ourselves from pain, and hurt caused by someone or something else in the past. She would talk about how difficult it was to take them down, but she knew she had to eventually. But I don't believe she realized that she already was. It was a natural thing, in those moments, together, in the work shop, or in the pool, or working on a project or even just lying in bed. Those walls were gone whenever we were together. Maybe not all but most. The problem was that they would go back up the second we were apart. Which was during the week. Most every week. II began to see this pattern developing. All week long she would find something to give me hell about, or complain about, or something she didn't like about what I did or didn't do. At times there was absolutely nothing I could do or say in her eyes that was going to be right. (Which is not to say she wasn't occasionally right). But on Friday I would pack up my dog Tucker, and head to her house, and when I got there and we saw each other. There really was no speaking or explaining necessary. All was right in the world again when we were together. Week after week we endured this. It became an endless cycle. She would get mad about something, most times she would use something I supposedly said several months before, as an excuse to be mad at me. And I would try to understand but inevitably I would get pissed, and lash out at how crazy she was. And say something that once again she would use against me. And any time we tried to talk about it the cycle would show itself, She would say "I'm mad because you did this" and of course my response would be..."Well I did that because you did this" and the circle would go on and on. Most times I had no idea why she would attack me. Or us, and at times I swear she just plain made shit up.

As the time went on it was clear to me. We only really had one problem, well ok 2 problems. Time. And Communication. She knew exactly how to push my buttons to get whatever response she needed. And she did it regularly. I once asked her just stop and talk to me. Just talk to me like an adult, calm. And see how much different results come from that approach vs attack mode or the silent treatment where I was left to guess what the problem was this time.

She finally did that one day. She called and I let her talk as long as she was calm and respectful. I listened to her every concern about, as was usual, something I had supposedly said month and months earlier. When she was done talking, I explained what I could, and apologized for what I couldn't. I also explained that it wasn't exactly fair to just pull something from months ago that no one remembers so I can't even defend myself, so she can just unload on me. When it was all done. She admitted she didn't expect the conversation to go that well, and whatever that situation was, was dealt with. I felt amazing after that conversation. I felt like we had just made a breakthrough, in learning to communicate with each other and a good portion of our issues would now be handled in a much better way.

Nope. Long story short, she inadvertently proved me right. She never would have even tried to have that calm conversation if she would have known it would be productive. She expected me to blow my top when she pushed those buttons, and then she could say....see, I told you. But that didn't happen. And from that conversation on, she never tried to communicate like that again. She knew the solution to the communication problem and refused it. It was at this time I started to realize that something else was going on here. It became clear that she was actively TRYING to sabotage our relationship. But as always, this was only while we were apart. When I would come to her house on the weekends we were fine. Loving and just happy to be in each other's arms again. But when I was getting ready to leave, the tension would start to mount. Her because she knew we were going to be apart for another week. I knew this too, but my tension was more so because I could see the switch about to take place in her. From loving partner to holy hell what am I going to have to deal with this week? Eventually it happened before I even left her house on Sunday.

The softer Louise became harder and harder to see. For every firecracker of a problem I caused, she would set off a pipe bomb. I became afraid to say or do anything. I couldn't try to talk to her because she would use anything I said against me. The real trouble started when we would argue on the phone. She would cry. And the kids could tell. All they knew was that mom was crying and it's because of Patrick. Over time the kids began to withdraw from me. I told Louise many times that she needs to either keep our conversations private or explain to the kids it not just Patrick being a jerk to their mom. I knew they were sensitive to this given the hell they watched her live through with her ex-husband. And I knew that Louise was the queen of "I never said…" She didn't tell the kids I was being a jerk or mistreating her. But she did let them see and hear her arguing. And crying. And in doing so, knew the kids would distance themselves from me, technically without her having to say a word. Just one more layer to the self-sabotage. And it worked.

Now obviously I would be remiss to try and make you the reader believe this was 100 percent on her. It wasn't. We had trust issues that developed on both sides. I believe out of fear of losing each other.

Scars from the past, both hers and mine. And for my part I know I didn't always do the right thing to alleviate the problem. Or say the right things to ease the tension. But to be honest, it came to a point that I really was scared to do anything at all, For fear of how she would act.

I could give countless examples of both of our short comings. That's not what this book is about. And I only write this chapter as an illustration of the extreme high of our love, and the plunge into darkness that came after. In Part 2 I will explain how all this fits into the Twin Flame journey. But please understand that this is in no way an attempt at using this book as a vessel to humiliate or air dirty laundry. Throughout all that has been written and all that is to come, my love for Louise has never wavered. And I believe her love for me hasn't wavered either. And I will do my best to explain soon.

Chapter 7

So far our journey has taken us to about the summer of 2016. Somehow we held on. For me I can say it was never a question of whether we should end it or not. Only, what can I do to fix it. Despite all the troubles and the attempts to sabotage this, I still loved her beyond all explanation. I knew what, in part, she was trying to do. Even if she wasn't aware. If she could drive me to the end of my rope I would leave. If she could make me do that she wouldn't have to. Because she couldn't. In fact the more I stayed, the more I tried to fix not run, the more she loved me, and the more fear over took her. I know, it's a strange concept, but if you are in a Twin flame relationship, you probably have no problem understanding.

Our love was still obvious. And for all the firecrackers and pipe bombs, all the dumb words that came out of my mouth in frustration, we were still wildly in love. But as the issues escalated, I became more and more fearful as well. What was she doing when she would disappear and give me a wild crazy excuse as to why? She knew I had always had a concern about her oldest and best friend wanting her to constantly spend time with her. You see, this woman had a whopper of a reputation. And on top of that, was known to actively participate in helping her other friends cheat on their spouses. So I did not ever feel secure when Louise was with this woman. And with our relationship seemingly deteriorating right before my eyes, spending more and more time with this woman was driving me crazy. But the more I expressed my concerns, the more time she spent with her. It was as if she had finally found that button that would lead to our downfall and she was pushing that button for all she was worth. All the while twisting it making it my fault. And in the end. Everything I was afraid of, came true.

But before that, I had been really turning to God, the Universe, Spirit guides, anything searching for the answers. How do I save this? How do I fix this? I began focusing on me. Not in a selfish way, but more to the fact that I realized trying to control Louise was never going to happen, no matter how positive my intentions. I could only control me and my part. And I knew despite all the hell she put me through, I was not without blame and fault. I could have and should have handled certain situations differently. In a better way. But can tell you even today looking back. Even if I had been perfect. She was hell bent on destroying us. It wouldn't have mattered. I began to know exactly what she was doing as far as trying to elicit a reaction from me. And I would do the opposite. I knew by this time that she was trying to get me to argue, and in doing so she could turn it on me and use it as justification for whatever it was she really wanted. Pipe bomb. But by this time I was on to it. And I also knew she loved me. Ironic and to some unbelievable, but it's true. I can't tell you how, but I started to become aware of the energy shared between us. I became aware that I can feel her. I knew if she was sad, or happy. I knew if she was heartbroken, or scared. What I didn't know was why I knew. Every time I would begin to feel down or hopeless concerning our relationship, I would remind myself of the positive we had shared. And the doubt would go away. I didn't realize it at the time but I was raising my energy and vibration by remembering the love and examples of it and in a way reliving it.

To my surprise, the simple act of not giving her the expected response, and doing my best to raise my energy through the positive, improvement seemed to be happening. There was a situation where I was supposed to attend a wedding for her niece with her. Long story short, she found a way to go without me and not actually have to tell me. That day on several occasions, she tried to solicit an angry response from me. I wasn't having any part of it. Every time I would just say, "Its fine dear, we can do anything you want" or "it's up to you dear, I set aside the entire day for you". It was so surprising to her that she actually asked me why I was being so nice. Nothing she was doing was working. Finally she told me not to come she was just going to drive her daughter over and leave. She wasn't going to stay and attend the wedding on account of some slight against her father who wasn't invited. She said she would just drop the daughter off and then come to my house as we had originally planned. I simply asked her if she was sure, and ok if that's what she wanted then I couldn't wait to have her with me.

Well, the hours rolled on, and of course no Louise. I tried to text her and got no response. Finally about 11:00 pm. She called and said she had just left. And she knew it was late so if I wanted, she could just go home and come to my house in the morning. I asked her what took her so long, knowing full well she just lied to me and found a way to attend this wedding without me on her arm, and the paranoid me wondered if she actually attended with a different date. But I kept my cool and didn't let on my fear. She gave me some crazy story about her mother and cooking potatoes. I told her that I was more than accommodating for her all day, and thanks to her I had sat waiting all day just to see her, so no I didn't want her to just go home I wanted her here with me. For the first time she couldn't even argue. I got a short sigh, and she said she would have to stop home and change. That was the first red flag. Change out of what? She had told me she wasn't going to attend the wedding, why would she need to change? Eventually, she did show up at my house. I had a beer waiting for her as was our custom when we would arrive, but instead of handing it to her I couldn't even look at her, something in me knew she was lying to me and the lies weren't over yet. I just told her with my back to her as she walked through the door, the beer was on the table, she would later use that against me because I didn't hand it to her. But in retrospect, I think she knew right then and there I was on to her, and what really happened.

WE talked and she did her best to give me a made up story about what took her so long. She even went on about having a flat and how impressed she was with a group of country boys as she called them fixing her tire for her. Red flag number two. This had nothing to do with anything, and the fact that she went on and on about it told me she was covering for something in case something should come out later. But I just let her go on.

I tried to act as if nothing was wrong. When it came time to go to bed, she changed and came into the bedroom dressed as if she was sleeping outside in February, Multiple layers, sweat pants and a sweatshirt, socks, every inch of skin from the chin down covered. It was July. Message was clear. Red flag number 3.

As she crawled into bed and put her cloths on the dresser, I could see her bra she had just taken off. Looked brand new. And after 4 years I knew what she had and what she wore to what. This wasn't an everyday undergarment. And I mentioned it and she did her best to blow it off, but I could see that twinkle of panic. Red flag number 4

As we sat in bed my mind was racing, it was clear she had lied and was continuing to lie, but why. As she sat there she had already put her hair up in a bun before she got to my house. But not the usual way. Normally it's what she called a messy bun, just hair kind of tied up. But tonight it was different. Scrunchies and bobby pins in it. And when she realized I noticed this nice strand of her blonde hair came undone and it was all curled nicely, she immediately went into lie mode. I didn't even have to say a word and she went on about how she found a new way to do her hair and put it up and then pull the strands down or whatever the line of crap was. But I didn't react. It was red flag number 5 and she had only been there for about an hour.

I turned the light off and we laid down. She was dressed for the artic so she didn't cover up with the blankets, but she rolled away from me. As I laid there on my back, mind racing trying to make sense of any scenario that would prove what I already knew to be true, wrong, she reached for me with her leg. I don't know if it was habit or instinct, or guilt. But it struck me as odd. I laid there and dozed off in confusion and hidden pain of knowing she had found an out. Most likely another man. I'm not saying that at this time she had physically cheated on me, but emotionally?

As I laid there in my sleep something woke me. I don't know what it was. But when I opened my eyes it was 3:00 am. And there was a light in the room. I instantly knew it was coming from Louise's phone she was leaned over the edge of the bed texting. At 3:00 am. I rolled over quickly on top of her and caught her on her phone. She panicked and swiped the phone clear so I couldn't see, while saying, its nana, its nana, I was talking to nana.. Her voice was panicked and clearly lying. She was trying to tell me she was talking to her then 15 yr. old daughter at 3:00 am. No, not this time, this was enough and all the proof I needed. I just said uh huh, right. And rolled over and never touched her again. I knew it was over. But I didn't know why she was there with me though. Regardless, I did my best to go to sleep.

The next morning, she never even tried to bring up the phone, or show me that she had been actually talking to her daughter and not someone else. She just sat in the bay window overlooking the pool. I made her coffee. In a last ditch effort I walked to her and tried to kiss her but she turned her head. I playfully asked her if she wanted to get naked. And she turned her head and looked me dead in the eyes, and said "No thanks, I'm good". I knew it. It was a swift kick in the balls. Like she spit in my face. She knew my pain and thoughts.

She knew, I knew she was guilty and did nothing, didn't even care enough to try to talk her way out of it.

Shortly after that, she made some excuse and left. I didn't speak another word to her. That was the last time I would see her as a couple.

Chapter 8

I had to stop and take a break. Writing that last chapter was difficult for me. Just as I said I can raise my vibration and energy by remembering and reliving the positive, the opposite is true when you dwell on the negative. Energy follows your thoughts. That's something to keep in mind. No matter the place you are at in your life.

And I have to clarify, and reiterate right here and now. As I said at the beginning of this writing adventure, I am writing this from my perspective as it happened to me. My experiences in the role that I have played thus far in this twin flame journey. Whenever possible as you've seen from previous chapters, I include what I know to be true of Louise's perspective as she has shared it with me. But as has been true with the last chapter, and many moving forward, she has not shared anything of her thoughts on what I described and detailed in the previous chapter. She has never addressed the 3:00am texting in my bed. She has never addressed what really happened that night, both at my house, or before she arrived. The only thing she has said in regards to that night is that if she ever got another chance, she would never ever do that to me again. Never treat me that way, and certainly never come to our bed dressed the way she was. But that's all that was said. No admissions or denials of anything. In a way I guess you could say it was an admission that she was doing it on purpose to hurt me, and she knew it. Why would she tell me she would never do that to me again through tearful eyes?

And in full disclosure, so much happened in such a short period time following, that I have never asked her or brought up that night to her in hopes of hearing the truth, or understanding. Maybe someday.

But as we move forward, some readers may feel that I am portraying her as a villain, or myself as a victim. For sure that is in no way my intention. I have a much better understanding now than when these events actually took place, as to what forces were at work, what lessons were to be learned on my part. And that these lessons could not be learned unless separation occurred. And any separation is never a good or pleasant experience.

I also can look back and say that I believe on some soul level she knew this too. Maybe not then, I don't know, but we will dive deeper into this in part two.

At this point in time it is July 2016. We had been together for just under 4 yrs. Before the fateful night I detailed in the previous chapter, I had been struggling with what our future may be. I say struggle because as I stated before, neither of us had any idea what was happening to us. She would later tell me that even she didn't understand why she did some of the things she did. The way we were at this point to an outsider, had to look like we were toxic to each other. But to us it was killing us inside, and neither would let go. In fact up until the night of the wedding, we were both holding on with all we had, yet still couldn't stop the freight train of despair. It was not only confusing as hell for us both, but I think we literally began to question our own sanity. I know for sure I did. And again, neither of us had any idea what a twin flame was.

In the weeks leading up to the night of her nieces wedding, things had begun to calm down a bit. At least from my perspective. I would later find out she was lying to me and sneaking out with her friend drinking and dancing and she even later admitted she had been hit on and in asked out by other men. All while I had no clue she was even going out.

Anyway, I thought things may be getting better. I had adopted the attitude of, I really don't care about being acknowledged as being right. The ego aspect was diminishing. Being right wasn't the important thing to me anymore, not in the big picture. That alone had allowed me to look at our issues and life in general with whole new perspective. And not realizing what she had been doing, I went and designed and bought her an engagement ring. At the time, as I said I believed things were getting better. And I knew I wanted to be her husband. I guess the only way to explain it is like I used to tell her,
"Just because you piss me off doesn't mean I don't love you, it just means you pissed me off."
In hind sight, maybe this wasn't the best idea I had. But as I found out was the normal, I didn't have but a fraction of the information. But again, this was all before the night of the wedding.
Ok, let's get back to the story...

Chapter 9

As I watched her drive away my heart
pounded. I knew she was never coming back.
I knew that, not for the first time, I had lost a
woman to another man. I noticed she never
stopped and looked back. She just left.

To be honest I don't remember much of the
following couple days. I went back to work and
tried to continue with my normal routine. She
knew I would call at lunch time and normally
she would call me in the morning on my ride
to work, I can't remember if she continued to
do that or not, but I did. I was hanging on by
the skin of my teeth. I felt she knew, that I
knew what had happened that night. But it
was never spoken of.
The days went by that week. We had spoken
at lunch time as normal, but not about
anything important, and things were at least
civil. I was lost in what to do. Was it over?
Should I address the elephant in the room? If
I didn't she would certainly just keep up
whatever it was she had going on the side
with someone else.

Even if it hadn't turned physical yet. I'm sorry it's cheating. But then again why is she still holding on to me. Why doesn't she just end it? Is she trying to have her cake and eat it too? There was of course the possibility that I was completely wrong. But if I was then why wouldn't she prove me wrong or even make an effort to ease my mind. In short, she couldn't.

She told me she was going to go to the psychic with the friend she knows I despise. Going to this place was sort of our thing. I had been the one to take her there the first time. So to me it was a bit of a kick in the nuts for her to take the one person I couldn't stand her being with. But she went and I didn't make a big deal out of it. She did call me on my lunch because she missed my call. Told me a little about the reading which had told her that the man that was drawn to the water was her forever man. Well. That was clearly me. And even she at that time acknowledged it. But the conversation was short, and that was that.

The next day she was nowhere to be found at lunchtime. Eventually she contacted me towards the end of the day, and I was not real happy. Things were starting to pile up on my mind and my heart, and I asked her why, for almost 4 years I called her at the same time every day, would you not be available today? What were you doing? And you know, I never did get the answer to that question. Instead she blew up at me. Listing all the things she hated about me, every little thing I ever said and or did, no matter how minor or insignificant, and never once did she tell me where she had been or what she had been doing to miss my call. This was Thursday. Friday came and it was more of the same. She disappeared all day and then would contact me at the end of the day, only now she didn't even call. It was nothing but text. And the same things she had blasted me for the day earlier. I couldn't understand, and didn't want to return the act and start firing back at her all the shit she had put me through. She had told me she wasn't coming to my house this weekend and didn't want me to come there, and went silent. That was Friday

By now it did not escape me that she clearly did not want to answer the question of where she had been 2 days earlier. And now she had plans to do something else and this time was making no mistake, making it clear she did not want me around.

I'm not too proud to say I was enraged. Which was exactly what she wanted. At this point, she was doing things to hurt me intentionally. And not knowing and then being ignored was the quickest way to get me to flip out. And she knew it.

The following day, she had gone on a kayak trip down the river in her town, with of course the woman that would do anything to break us up. And several others who to this day I couldn't tell you who. I tried and tried all day to contact her and all I got back was that she was on the river service wasn't good. And then silence. Of course I was pissed beyond any comprehension. My mind raced, who was she with? It had to be the man from the night of the wedding. And now everyone there with her knew she was mine, and were laughing at me while she played with him.

I was not in any way thinking clearly, tears filled my eyes and I was so enraged that I was throwing things. The only resemblance of control I had was not to drive over and find her with someone else and confront them both, because I wanted to, the only thing that stopped me was her kids. I didn't know where they were, or if they were with her and whoever else.

Eventually she returned home and began texting, she didn't want to talk, she was busy, had invited all the people over for a get together at her house. That was code for there's a guy in the group and if there's lots of people here it won't be obvious. She texted me to stay away, she don't have time for this, It's over.

She actually said the words. I was stunned. I couldn't move. My knees buckled and I dropped to the floor. Sobbing like a little kid. Right there in my living room, while she was enjoying a party with someone else. She told me right then and there later, that she looked down on the counter at 2 feathers she had found on her kayak trip that day. And shrugged and went out the door to her guests.

She put her phone down and went on to whatever it was that she actually did that night. To this day I don't know. But I do know she wouldn't have actually said the words unless she had found something else she wanted.

I went off the deep end. And let me tell you it wasn't pretty. I called about 40 times. Cell phone, home phone, left messages on the answering machine. Filled her voice mail box, texted constant. In her frame of mind then, I pictured her as laughing at me, sharing my pain with all her guests, and using my actions as an excuse to justify what she had done. No one knew the whole truth but her. Not even me.

I called again and again, and got the idea to check her voice mail, a trick I had used before, but I didn't know her password. But I tried every birthdate and number combination I could. I never did get it, but apparently she got a message from the phone company that someone had several missed attempts. And that's when she responded, I don't even remember what the response was, but we all know it wasn't nice. I had called her a cheater, several times a liar, told her what a shitty role model she was being for her daughter. The only response I got was....I never cheated. Problem was her definition of cheating is very fluid. Just because you haven't let him put his cock in you yet don't mean you didn't cheat. And I think I said that to her. But again, I blew up. All the things I was holding inside came out, via text because this was the beginning of what still goes on today, lots of text. She refuses to hear my voice.

I drank myself into oblivion that evening, and passed out. I knew it was the only way I would sleep and the only way the hurt would stop, even for a little while. To say I was completely devastated was a severe understatement. And yet I can't even say I didn't see it coming. But you'd have thought I got hit by a bus. I was nonfunctional. Meaning I couldn't even get out of bed. I don't mean I didn't want to, I mean I couldn't physically. I rolled everything over and over in my mind, and still couldn't make sense of anything. Not only what she had done, which I may never know what she did to the whole extent. I don't know who she was with, who she may have woke up with, kissed, screwed in the barn, or if there was no one there she was interested in and nothing happened. I can only draw my own conclusions based on her actions because she to this day has never told me the whole truth.

But what I did know was how I handled myself. I did know I went off the deep end, and I don't even blame the alcohol. I wasn't proud of myself and in fact I was ashamed. Regardless of whatever she had done to me I should never have handled myself in that manner.

Later that night, I sent her an email apologizing for my reaction. I did my best to tell her how devastated I was, but it didn't matter and I knew it. I told her I was ashamed of myself for acting that way, and the only way I knew to prevent future issues, was to delete her contact info from my phone. That way I couldn't ever bother her again even if I wanted to. I was so distraught and completely defeated I didn't even know how to feel or think or what to do next.

And that was only the beginning.

Chapter 10

In the days that followed, I was a wreck.
Doing my best to hold it together, if for
nothing else, I didn't want my kids to see me
this way. Luckily my daughter and my son
were gone to their mothers for a week. A bit
of a double edge sword. Good that I had some
time to try to get myself composed, but bad
because I was left all alone to deal with the
worst days of my life.

I am not one to go tell everyone what
happened. I don't like people knowing my
business and am in fact a very private person.
Even now I was protective of Louise in the
sense that I didn't want anyone else to know
what had happened and in my mind what she
had done to me. Not because of
embarrassment, but because I didn't want
anyone thinking badly of her. So I kept all of
the pain and suffering to myself. I had no
other choice. And the emotions were in my
opinion, literally killing me.

A couple days later she emailed me back. Not exactly sure what the email said. But I know in my mind she didn't have to do that. So I viewed it as a reach for me on her part. It wasn't, it was just the way I saw it at the time. And of course I asked repeatedly how she could do this to me. I asked her repeatedly to just tell me if there was someone else. To which she never once gave a straight answer. Of yes or no. I asked and asked, and to be honest, yes, knowing the truth would have helped my understanding of what the hell happened. But also, it would have been the end of it. Had she told me yes there is/was someone else, id have disappeared. But she knew this too. So she never would say.

She later told me that she began "going places and doing things". And that's how she met new people. Well, that's not exactly how it happened. That's just what she was telling me. I mean come on, You don't just randomly walk up to a group and crash it. You don't just magically all of the sudden have a dozen friends who you have never once in 4 years even mentioned. Yet that's what she wanted me to believe. But that doesn't exactly explain much. My guess would be these are people she met at the wedding and that was through whoever the man was. But even as I write this I have to say, I have no idea what the truth is because she has never said. And in my opinion never will. The only thing I do know is that what she was telling me WAS NOT the truth.

After about a week, I was doing my best to leave her alone. No phone calls, no text. I had blocked her and deleted her contact info to prevent that. The only option for her to communicate with me was email. And looking back, no matter how hard I tried to give her what she wanted, she would find a way to contact me, or should I say a reason. About 1 month after she left, she still was holding fast to never ever telling me the truth. And never answering a single question. She decided to contact me and ask me for some tools she had given me. I couldn't believe it. I agreed to meet her where they were stored, and she came. While it was the single most emotional day I had ever experienced. She down played it. Even though we both were in tears before we even saw each other, and the first thing she did was run to me and put her arms around me and cry on my chest. She still later said it was just because of where we were. I begged of course for a reunion. I asked face to face if there was someone else and face to face she said no. But the lie was given away by the shirt she was wearing. It was a shirt from an event a man on her social media site frequented. And absolutely nothing that she ever expressed any interest in. and although when I asked her, she denied it. Said it was just something she did with a group of friends. But for some reason it was clear she was lying. She would later tell me that she went way out of her way to ensure she wasn't tagged in any pictures together with him on social media. She did not want me to know. She claimed it was because she didn't want to hurt me, but it was much more than that. More time went on and again I did my best to leave her alone. And at times I did well, at others not so much. The holidays came and around that time I had asked her to go to see a counselor with me. She of course never would answer even that question until I was sitting in the councilor's office.

I had tried so hard to move on. But nothing I tried ever mattered. I could not stop loving her. And for the life of me I couldn't figure out why. I was on the brink of crashing hard. I mean snapping and god knows what next. I was having trouble even functioning throughout the day because my mind was all encompassed with her. On a suggestion from a coworker I decided to try to go to counseling. It was something Louise had in fact suggested in the past, but I declined. I didn't believe she would give it her all. And tell the whole truth to even the councilor. At that time she would have even tried to manipulate the councilor by telling only the part that made her the victim. So I declined. But now I'd try anything. I searched for a councilor on line and found a few, but I was uneasy. But then I came across a page that had Kate listed. I chose her because of her eyes. As I had said before, I believe you can see right through someone if you can look them in the eye. This was in no way because she's beautiful. Obviously I was still so madly in love with Louise. But something about her called to me. I just knew. I called and left a message and when she returned my call, I explained briefly over the phone that I wanted the couples counseling, but if she didn't show up it would revert to single therapy with the goal of getting past this. She agreed and we set an appointment. For the next week I did pester Louise through email, and by now she and I had gotten past the road block with the phone. But I wouldn't use that. The day of the appointment came and I walked in and met Kate. As I sat down she asked if Louise was coming. I told her no. She knew the time and didn't show, and my intention now was an explanation as to why all this time goes by and I am no better than the day she left. Our first appointment was November 17th. And I saw Kate once a week. Her focus was on figuring out why I still give energy to Louise after all she has put me through. I explained I don't know. I wished I could just be like everyone else and just move on. I explained and Kate agreed that this was no ordinary everyday relationship. In fact it was something much deeper and spiritual. And it was Kate's confirmation of what I already knew that made me decide to start researching what the hell was happening. And it was Kate that suggested I research Empaths. She recognized that I was empathic but felt it was better for me to figure that out on my own, so she guided me to the discovery.

All this time, the challenge for Kate was to get me to stop giving my energy to Louise. She had her hands full. Every minute of the day I was thinking of her. And I was stalking her social media as well. Basically just to feel connected to her still in some way. And I would later find out Louise was doing the same thing. And still making sure no picture of her and him were posted or tagged for me to see. This was months after she left. Clearly she was starting to understand that this wasn't something we could run from.

But although I was checking her social media, I had forced myself to not contact her in any way. It had been just over a month. I had not reached for her. I wasn't getting over her. I was just becoming numb to the pain. And doing my best to occupy my thoughts with not so much how to get her back, but how to move forward. Why I can't stop loving her. Lord knows I had every reason to never speak to her again. And I was on my way to that, even though it wasn't what I wanted. I began to question my own sanity. Was I just in some way obsessed? It didn't feel that way to me. I was doing my best to give her what she wanted. And I was doing better. I could get through a day without crying. I could make myself go through a week without reaching for her.

It was nine days before Christmas. About 11:00 pm. On a Saturday night. I was sitting in my chair, alone in the house. I instantly had this overwhelming feeling of Knowing. I can't explain any better, it was sort of like a panic attack that got worse by the second. My heart was racing, and all that my mind was focusing on was I got to call I got to call now call now call now! I fought this feeling knowing I had come so far and hadn't tried in over a month, and why now! I haven't heard her voice since she came to get the tools. Some 4 months before. I had of course tried to call but she never once answered, why should now be any different. But the panic attack like sensation would only intensify by the second. I reached for my phone thinking ill just call, she won't answer as usual and that will be that. But to my surprise, she did answer, and the second she did the panic attack was gone.

I was dumbfounded. I never in a million years expected her to answer. And was upset with myself for calling, but the feeling that came over me suddenly was one of urgency, as if I didn't have a choice. I knew she needed me. I could not at the time, explain why or how I knew.

We talked for over 2 hours that night. For the first time in so long we just talked and as was in the beginning, the conversation just flowed. We weren't laughing and joking but I was so stunned I didn't want the call to end. And I know she felt the same.

5 minutes after she answered, she was in tears. I honestly don't know why. I think it was the guilt she was feeling. It was 9 days before Christmas, and she had in a sense fallen into a state of depression. Normally she goes so crazy overboard spending on the kids for Christmas, but now she told me its 9 days away and she had not bought one thing yet. Even she knew this wasn't her normal self. She will never tell you but it was as if she had finally realized what she had done. She was hurting in that moment for whatever reason, and thinking of me. And that triggered the pull on me to call. Later we would discuss that night. And she would admit. Yes that night she did need me. Though she stops short of giving me the details of why.

Anyway, towards the end of the conversation I asked her if she would have dinner with me. Just start over with another first date. She was silent. I asked if she was silent because she was seeing someone. And her response was,

"Well, sort of, we've been on a few dates but it's nothing serious. But I'll have to have a conversation with him first"

"I don't understand "I said. "If it's nothing serious why do you have to have a conversation with him?"

She said she felt she would have to let him know that we had talked and that she wanted to follow this opportunity and see where it goes.

I asked her how it is not serious if she feels the need to talk to him first.

Her response was

"It's just a whatever whenever type of thing, obviously it's not very serious, if I'm home alone on a Saturday night"

And that reminded me so much of the random acts of kindness remark she used way back in the beginning. And I was upset. Clearly she wasn't happy, and obviously this other man was more than she was letting on. But I didn't push in anger. I didn't want to waste this opportunity. I told her point blank

"Why would you ever allow someone to make you nothing but a whenever whatever girl. Do you realize that's nothing more than admitting you are nothing but a booty call?"

She didn't respond. So I told her

"Please Louise, I am asking you point blank with no pretense, if this other man is just whatever whenever, then I am asking you to end it. And agree to come on a date with me and give us a chance to see what happens"

She agreed to my surprise. She said she would talk to him on Sunday, and after that we could plan a date. I was over the moon happy but I was trying so hard not to show it. Before we got off the phone I asked her if she would at least keep in contact and not disappear in the meantime. She agreed. And told me she would call me when t was done. I thanked her. And we hung up.

I ran out the door and screamed at the top of my lungs! And then dropped to my knees and gave thanks for answering my prayer. I went to sleep that night with hope in my heart that I wasn't crazy after all. It did matter that I held on. And it wasn't all for nothing.

Sunday came and went, Louise didn't call. I was pacing waiting but didn't want to push too hard. I take that back, I really wanted to push but knew I shouldn't. Monday came and all day I had hoped to hear from her. It wasn't until about 7:00 that evening, she called. She was hiding from her kids, because she didn't want them to know she was talking to me. But she said that she hadn't had the chance to have the conversation with him yet. But she wanted to call because she had said she would. I asked her when she was going to get this taken care of, and she told me that Wednesday she would talk to him. She said she had to go but she would talk to me soon. And hung up.

Soon never came. She never called back. I can only assume she either never tried to talk to him, or she did try and he convinced her not to come back to me. Either way, she disappeared again. And I tried so hard again to contact her.

I couldn't understand how in the course of a day or two she could flip flop like that. As if she could just hit a switch and turn her feelings on and off. Robotic almost.

Once again I was devastated. When I saw Kate, I explained the feeling I had and the reason I called, and the outcome. She explained to me the reason I had that feeling was because of the connection between us. It was so strong that I can feel when she is happy, or sad, or in trouble, or in need. And that just because I can feel her, doesn't mean I have to respond. And at the time I thought Kate was wrong. To me, the way I felt, I had no choice. The panic that was instant was so immeasurably strong and getting stronger every second until I called and it was immediately gone.

What I would come to understand later, through Kates guidance and some research I had done on my own, was that she was right. I just wasn't strong enough yet to choose not to respond to the draw from Louise's energy. But I was learning. And the more I learned the stronger I got. And the more I pulled my energy and effort away from Louise, the more she held on tight to it. She too could feel when I was pulling away. But she didn't know what it was or why she was feeling it. I did. It was becoming more understandable. At least the part about the energy shared between us. Though I still didn't know why. Why was it, that I was cursed this way? Almost as if I was sentenced to a life of misery, and never being able to move on. I was still in constant pain, which has never stopped. I was simply learning to deal with the pain.

Chapter 11

I was "awakening" so to speak. I just didn't realize it yet. I was still in agony over losing Louise, and now having to deal with the fact of knowing she is moving on, and leaving me behind only added to my misery. To this point I had prayed every day for her. For her strength and courage to do what was right. I knew she was still in love with me. I could feel it. And I felt amazingly stupid for feeling this way, when everything in the world told me otherwise. I prayed for strength to do whatever was necessary on my part to help facilitate her return.

I was going to Lily dale to seek guidance as well. And amazingly most of what I was told was in line with what Kate was telling me. Kate had introduced me to Energy, and the shared energy, and the fact that there is energy in everything. Being an Empath, which was a new revelation for me as well, we are much more in tune with this energy, and the fluctuations involved. We tend to take on the energy of the people around us, in short, we don't just mentally understand what someone is saying, and we can actually feel what they are feeling. Good, bad, joy, pain, anxiety, deceit, anger, you name it. It is absorbed by Empathic people. Because of this, some common traits of Empaths, are things like, being able to read people like a book, and in seconds. Knowing when someone is lying to you before the words ever come out of their mouths. Experiencing very high highs, and very low lows. Just to name a few that apply here.

I was having trouble dumping the negative energy once it was absorbed. But I was an open vessel to all of her energy, good or bad. And in return, she was an open vessel for mine. The only difference is, I now knew it. She hadn't been awakened to this knowledge.

The lily dale healer, explained to me more about our spirit guides and how everyone has them. Some people understand this and others do not. Most everyone has heard of the concept of spirit guides, but most don't seek any knowledge concerning them.

She recommended a book for me to read to get better acquainted with the concept. So I went out and bought it, and read it cover to cover. The thing that stood out the most to me in the reading was the explanation of the energy flow between 2 people, and how energy follows thoughts. But also how this energy can be used.

While I was still in agony, over Louise, I was at least learning, slowly what the hell was going on. I had not heard from Louise in any way since she disappeared. Christmas came and went. As did New Year's day. Shortly after that, it was a Sunday, and I was home alone. Again sitting in my chair. It was morning time because I had just made my coffee. I was I admit, still stalking her social media page, and by now she knew it. And could in fact put things on there she knew I would see. Or hide things and only share them with everyone but me. I honestly still just wanted to feel connected to her in some way. But as I sat in my chair, I felt the same urgency I had felt before. The same panic. But this time it more as if something was wrong. I picked up my phone, and instead of calling her, I went to her Facebook page and there it was. Only 3 minutes earlier, she had changed her relationship status. It now said she was in a relationship with this other man. I saw this and jumped to my feet. Heart pounding, and I felt a sharp pain like I never experienced shoot from my abdomen up the center of my chest. It was so sharp and strong and sudden that it dropped me to my knees. I thought I was having a heart attack. But even in that pain, I couldn't think of anything but her. Just a few weeks ago she told me there was nothing serious. He was a whenever whatever

sort of thing. She had agreed to give us a fresh start. And now she's on the largest social media outlet in the world advertising her relationship. And not only that, but the people were commenting on it saying things like "It's about time" and
"I thought you have been for a long time"
All the comments confirmed that they had in fact been together for many, many months, and I had been right all along.

To say I lost control again was a bit of an understatement. I immediately emailed her asking what the fuck was wrong with her. And now I had proof she had been lying all along. I was not happy and devastated yet again.
And just to rub salt in the wound, she responded with an email telling me how she had never felt more loved. It was the kick in the balls and spit in the face. She knew it would hurt me. And that's why she said it. Yet she immediately hid the relationship status from public view.

From that day on I was done. Oh I hurt very badly. Seemed every time I turned around she was finding a new way to spit in my face. But even now I couldn't understand why. Why not block me on all platforms and cut the cord. Just be done? But she didn't. And the reason I began to realize was if she did then she couldn't check on me, and my life and what I was doing.

As she knew all along, once I knew for sure that she was in deed seeing someone else, I was gone. And that's exactly what I was. I from that day on didn't try to contact her in any way. I never wanted to be that other man. Even though he was and didn't mind. I wouldn't play that role. I disappeared as promised. It was only later that I would understand how much this hurt her, yet advanced her knowledge.

Chapter 12

Shortly after finding out about her new and supposedly wonderful relationship, I had decided I better at least check my health. I went to the doctors and had a bunch of blood work done, and turns out my cholesterol was through the roof. According to my doctor, that meant my blood was in essence, extremely thick. Which made my heart work a lot harder to pump. I asked her what caused this and she told me the usual things, diet, stress, and it's hereditary. Stress I thought?

I went on some prescribed cholesterol medication, and to be honest I didn't take it as I was instructed. Once in a while I would remember and take it. But that's about it. The more I talked with Kate and my contact at lily dale. The better I felt. I still missed Louise fiercely. But a few months went by and I had managed to not contact her in any way. And I hadn't heard from her either. I had resigned myself to the fact that she had moved on. It was only me that could not. It was becoming obvious in my mind that this was a one sided situation. She must be happy with her choice. And I'm still living with hopes of the past.

I was trying to move forward and I had read somewhere that forgiveness is needed to truly move on. So I began to think about this and wonder if true forgiveness is truly possible, and I came to a standstill when faced with the question my mind had conjured. What is the difference between True forgiveness, and just accepting something you can't change? I put this question to Kate. She of course was caught a bit off guard, and unprepared for such a philosophical question. It was kind of amusing to see the look on her face when she heard me ask it.

Anyway, the answer I came up with after several days of thought, and pondering, is this.

When you can be thankful for going through the experience that needs forgiving, you can offer true forgiveness. Until then, there will always be a little resentment and bitterness in you preventing you from truly forgiving someone.

That may not sit well with some readers, and some may disagree, and that's ok. For me, this was the lesson I needed to learn. And it begs the age old saying,
"It's better to have loved and lost, than never to have loved at all"

I was coming to terms with life without Louise. I still prayed for her every day, for her strength, courage, and for the lord to open her eyes. To clear space in her heart for us. I was in a sense, I thought, healing. Even if the wound would leave a massive scar.

I was embracing the role of the spirit guides. In my research I found that your guides are always with you. They will never leave. And they welcome the opportunity to communicate. You need only ask. They leave signs for you all the time. Trying to point you min the right direction, or maybe just to let you know you aren't alone and they are right there with you. It's up to you to understand the signs and see them for what they are. I decided to test this theory. I prayed and asked the guides for a sign. Something form Louise, some sort of undeniable sign that not only the guides were listening, but that I wasn't crazy, and she and I would be reunited.

I really didn't hold much hope for an actual response or sign. But at this point I was trying not only to learn, but to determine whether I really was just crazy in my belief that our story wasn't over. After saying the prayer, I wrote it down, and put it in a box that I had next to my bed. I also put in the box a feather. I'm not sure why, but the feather for some reason felt as if it meant something to me. I went upstairs to take a shower, and when I returned I checked my phone. No calls or text. I didn't really know how long this might take, and in fact regretted not using a specific time line as proof.

I decided to check my own Facebook page, and had recently changed my profile picture to one of my chocolate lab. After I was done on my page I of course switched over to check hers. And my heart skipped a beat at what I saw. Tears filled my eyes. I just sat there staring. In the time since I had said the prayer, Louise had gone online and changed her profile picture to one of her and her dog. A chocolate lab.

To me, It was not only proof that she was indeed checking my page as I was hers, but also the answer to my request for undeniable proof that the guides were listening, and I wasn't crazy to be holding on.

I know some of you readers will say it's a coincidence, and again, that's fine with me. The thing to understand is that your guides are not going to use signs that you personally don't understand to try to communicate. They will be signs that mean something to you personally. Just because it is a feather for me, doesn't mean it will be a feather for you. Maybe it's a penny, or a flower, it's whatever they know you will equate with them.

Later Louise would deny having knowledge of the picture I posted. But would in fact acknowledge that she did indeed do the same thing I was doing in stalking my page. After that I began asking questions of my guides and asking for specific things as confirmation. And using reasonable time lines to respond. The normal sign I equated with my guides was a feather. And since then I find feathers everywhere. Coincidence? No not to me. And no I don't look for them. They basically present themselves to me in the oddest places. After seeing the picture, I went to sleep that night, at least feeling as if I wasn't alone. And that I wasn't crazy after all. I had never lost my faith in her or us. Even after all that had happened. Just since the breakup. Some of the things I haven't written about that she has said to me, the hurtful times when it seemed she was going out of her way to show me how insignificant I had become.

Everything had to be forgiven. And I had grown in myself, to realize that.

As I slept, the most amazing thing was happening. I was being flooded with answers. Realizations, what to change, the effect of that change if I made it. Just a flood of information. And it felt like ecstasy. It felt wonderful and heartwarming to be given this information I didn't really even know I needed. I woke up and didn't move for a minute, making sure I remembered everything. I did, but not only that, it didn't stop when I woke up. The answers kept coming. In the form of thoughts, and feelings and emotions. I suddenly knew exactly what SHE felt like in certain situations, when before I was so focused on how terrible she made me feel. I suddenly understood what she meant when she would talk about time and her issues with me leaving her house on a Sunday. I realized exactly how simple it would have been to address that. Every issue that we had had for the entire time we were together, came into clarity. And while I was in utter amazement at what was happening, I also felt both excited to know exactly how to do things different, but also ashamed that I did or didn't do or say some of the things she needed me to do or say.

As I lay there awake, and still soaking in this information, I was smiling. I had a tear drawing down my cheek. And when it was over, I felt empowered. I had just learned so many lessons almost instantaneously. I knew exactly what to do next time. But then the realization hit me, I have no reason to believe there ever will be a next time. But I knew I had to try and improve myself.

I went back to lily dale to speak to my healer there, and she told me I had been given a wonderful gift from my guides. And that gift was knowledge. It wouldn't have been given if it were not necessary for growth, and to be used on my journey. She suggested that I go and, prepare my house so to speak. A metaphor, for work on these lessons and use this knowledge to prepare myself, for when the opportunity presented itself to use it.

Chapter 13

I had not heard anything from Louise in a couple of months. Though I still looked at her page. There were times when I knew she was sending me a message that only her and I would recognize. Once she posted a picture of her on the couch, wearing one of my sweatshirts. And she was staring into the camera, with no smile. The caption read something about the beach, which was our place. All generic to anyone else. No one knew that was my sweatshirt. But she did, and I did. And the reference to the beach was a simple statement everyone could relate to in the cold days of February, but she was looking straight into the camera and not smiling, speaking to me. Of course again, she would later deny ever trying to communicate in that manner with me. But I know better.

One day, I'd guess it was a Wednesday. Out of the blue she sent me an email. Imagine my shock to see her name attached, and to be honest I for a second didn't want to read it. Everything else had been so negative that I couldn't imagine this being any different. But of course I opened it.

In the message, she told me about a dream she had had a few nights prior, in which, she was simply standing there, and appeared a little ways off. I walked to her carrying a bouquet of daisies, her favorite flower. And as I approached, I handed her the flowers and smiled and said goodbye. And turned and walked away. As I walked away, she called for me, but no matter how much she called my name, I wouldn't turn around. And as she looked down at the beautiful flowers I had given her, they were dying. The farther I walked away, the more they died. Till eventually she was left with a bouquet of once beautiful flowers, which were now all dead. She went on to tell me that when she awoke, she felt happy for me for some reason. But she couldn't shake the meaning of the dream. I don't remember if she asked me what I thought it meant or not, but I'm not sure she really did awake feeling happy. I kind of think that was just thrown in there so I didn't think she wanted me to stay and wait for her. But she continued to write, that if in deed I had moved on that she was happy for me. And that was all she wrote.

After months she reached out to me. Because of this dream. She knows I believe dreams can be used to send messages, and can be very prophetic. So I responded.

I told her, that no, in fact I hadn't exactly moved on. But her dream was in fact a message from her guides. In effect showing her what was coming. The symbolism of the flowers. Her favorite, and she always complained about her exes buying her roses instead of what she wanted. I was the only one that paid enough attention and brought her daises. When I turned around and left. No matter how much she called after me, I wouldn't turn around. And the farther I walked away the more the flowers died. I don't know what there is to be happy for me about in that scenario. To me at that time, it simply said to her that she was killing the most beautiful thing ever given to her.

Now, my assessment of the dream may be off. I'm no expert. And I don't know if she told me everything about the dream or not. But it was powerful enough to get her attention. And while her mind may have somehow interpreted it as I had finally moved on, I don't think that's what she was really thinking. It's possible that she had this dream just as she described it, and was fearful that I had moved on, in the sense that I had found someone else. And the reason it affected her so much was that I wasn't chasing her anymore. She felt the energy change when I had that wonderful experience of enlightenment for lack of better term. But as of yet she still doesn't recognize what it is that affects her. But I believe she is starting to realize no matter what she does, or how hard she tries to burry herself into other things and other people. She cannot outrun or hide from whatever it is that we are.

As I said. My assessment of the dream may have been way off. But one things for sure. It was meant to tell her something. Whether I was told all the information about it or not only she can say. Maybe it was nothing but a way for her to reach out and make sure I was still right there waiting. Maybe it was both. I don't know.

Chapter 14

After the email concerning the dream, there were a few emails back and forth. I told her how I was learning and about the flood of information. I told her how after learning the true meaning of forgiveness I felt lighter and less burdened.

She went on to say that she too had learned several lessons, and learned much about herself, though she stopped short of explaining what it actually was that she learned.

I had asked her to please stop reaching for me. I told her we weren't going to be friends no matter how hard she tried to make us that. After all that we had been through friends just wasn't going to be close to enough for us ever. At the time she said ok. She agreed, and made out as if she was only doing it for me. But I knew it wasn't. it was for her. And just like the last time she had gone a while without me reaching for her, she had to try to pull me back. She wouldn't let go either. She just didn't want anyone to know it or have to admit it.

Don't misunderstand, I wanted her in my life so very badly. But I was recognizing that this little back and forth texting or email, were doing more harm than good, it was nothing more than a reach to make sure I was still there. She had no intentions of actually coming back. I was in affect her safety net. She could play with her new man all she wanted, and still string me along. It didn't take much. From the time she left I was begging for contact from her. And she was always the master at implying one thing and letting you believe it, and never delivering on what she made you believe. She always needed that out. "I never said..."

Now I was growing stronger. But more importantly I gaining knowledge every day. I was relying on my guides to show me through. I still had no idea what a twin flame was, but I knew that what was happening wasn't normal. I still prayed every day for her. And her courage and strength. But no matter how much I learned, or how strong I became, I'm still only human. There's still only so much one man can take before he breaks. I had my dark days, where I would curse god for making me suffer. For not letting me move on like a normal human would. I began to pray now, not for her courage. But that if he refused to put me in her heart, then please take her out of mine. I didn't want the hurt anymore. There was no end in sight. The more she felt for me, the farther she would run. The worse her decisions became. It was her way of dealing with the separation. The pain that she felt, but wanted no one to know.

As June approached, it weighed heavy on my mind, that not only my son was going to be graduating from high school, but her son as well. I hadn't spoken to any of her children since she left me. But I missed them more than I could explain. Especially her middle son who had become close to me. I wanted nothing more than to be there to see him graduate. But I knew that wasn't going to happen. One day I had just stopped and bought her son a graduation card and put some money in it, so at least he would know I remembered him. That same day my son had texted me from school, saying he just got a message from Louise. She had contacted him on social media telling him she had a gift for him for graduation, but didn't want to cause trouble so was it ok to give it to him. I had only told the kids that if they heard from her I wanted to know about it. I told Evan its fine. It's very nice of her to remember him, and he had his own car, he could make arrangements to meet her somewhere if necessary so he could pick it up and at least say thank you. But in reality I told him that knowing her, she would just pick a time when she knows you are at school and I'm at work and just drive over and drop it off for you.

I was exactly right. About a week later, the same day my card arrived for her son, she showed up at 3:30 after school, thinking the kids wouldn't be home. Louise and her daughter both came and pulled into the driveway. But Erin was home. She immediately called me and told me Louise was there and what should she do. I told her to relax, she's probably just dropping off a gift for Evan.

So Erin met them outside and shocked them both because they didn't think anyone would be home. Of course they said hello, and Louise marveled at how Erin had grown in the last year. Erin took the gifts and put them in Evans room for him. And Louise and her daughter were on their way.

One thing to add here is that as I stated earlier, I never told anyone what had happened between us. Only that we weren't together any more. I never wanted the kids or anyone else to think badly of her. And when she and I were together they loved her. So it meant so much to Evan that she went out of her way to make sure he knew she was thinking of him. Louise's gift giving was always unique. Her gifts genuinely came from the heart. She wasn't afraid to spend money, but the creative nature that resides in her always shined through. She also had her oldest son already in college and her middle son going into his first year just like Evan. So she had a very good grasp on what the kids would need and what would probably be forgotten or overlooked by a first timer like myself. I couldn't say she was wrong about that.

Evan got home about the same time I did. And was more excited than I would have expected. He went straight up stairs to his room to check out what Louise had left. And to be clear, this wasn't a... Happy kid on Christmas morning type of excitement. He was genuinely surprised and shocked that she remembered him. When he went into his room he found three baskets. One was a clothes basket loaded with laundry soap, shower supplies, I think she got him flip flops for shower shoes, all sorts of things like cold medicine, headache medicine, a little pouch of quarter for the laundry machine. You name it she thought of it. Another basket was full of things like pens and pencils, closet organizers, shower caddies, batteries, etc. And still another was loaded down with towels and wash cloths she had folded into volcano looking thing. Evan couldn't believe it. And as I stood next to him I told him to make sure he contacted her to say thank you. He just had this smile on his face and he said
"I love Shan........."
He stopped and looked at me as if he had just been caught betraying his dad. I just grinned and told him whatever our troubles are, they don't have anything to do with you. It's ok to Love Louise. I still do too.

It was clear that Louise had put a ton of time and effort into putting this together for Evan. You don't do that for someone you don't love. And that message came through loud and clear to Evan. To this day, he doesn't hear from her. It's not as if they kept in touch with each other after that. But he was grateful. Later that day, I received a message from her son, telling me thank you for remembering him and sending the card. For me I often wondered if that gift for Evan was in reality also an olive branch of sorts. I mean, why go to all that trouble and spend all that time and effort, if you haven't seen him in well over a year, and based on the decisions you've made, you may never see him again. I mean I get that she is a nice and thoughtful person, but a simple card would have had the intended effect. Don't misunderstand me, what she did was wonderful, and greatly appreciated. But if she really was done with me. Then why? I texted her later and told her thank you for remembering him. And told her how much it meant to him. She responded telling me that she only contacted him because she didn't know if I was with someone else and didn't wasn't to cause trouble.

To me, maybe I'm overthinking it, but by now I know the way she thinks, and that seemed to be a way to dig, and hope id tell her if I was or wasn't seeing someone else. Recognizing

this, I only responded with
"No trouble"

And left it alone. A few weeks later she had posted some pictures of her with her son on graduation night. I'm sure knowing I would see them. And I did the same with Evans. Of course, knowing she would see them.

Chapter 15

I had effectively stopped openly chasing her.
I wasn't contacting her in anyway. And when
she would reach for me I was short. Not giving
the information she seemed to be wanting. Or
I should say that I perceived that she wanted.
But just because I wasn't begging her every
day, didn't mean I didn't want her. I still loved
her more than life itself. And for whatever
reason I still believed in her, and knew that
she would find her way back. Even though I
had zero reason to have any faith at all. I just
did. Which also means that just because I
wasn't communicating with her, didn't mean I
had given up, and I was still sending her my
energy along with my love every day. And she
may not have recognized it but she felt it. And
every time she would feel it she would dig
herself in deeper to the whole she created to
hide.

She started posting things about "her new
home" and moving to a different town and
"goodbye town." The next thing you know the
house is posted on social media as being for
sale. Long story short, she was running again.
This time moving into the other man's home.
All being posted on social media, where she
knew I'd see.

I don't know why this wasn't enough to send me over the deep end once more. I hated it, don't get me wrong. But any sane man would realize this was the dagger to the heart. There was no coming back from this. I said any sane man.

I began to doubt myself again. I began to believe it was over for good. And then I happened to come across something called a Twin Flame, on the internet. This was described as the most powerful bond any human could have. God given, and extremely rare when to twin flames find each other. I went on to read that these two souls are actually 2 halves of the same soul. Eternally connected. I began to read more, and research more about this and I don't need to recap here because if you are reading this you are already familiar with what I found. I couldn't get enough information. It described US to a "T". Perfectly from start to present. To say I was amazed is putting it lightly.

I read more books and found everything I could on the internet about it and then tried to process what was happening. Basically, about a dozen books had just described perfectly, my life struggles of the past year. It spoke of synchronicities, and recognizing signs. It talked about what a runner was and why they run, and what the chaser was and why they chase. And the soul lessons that need to be learned. And how even though we are 2 parts of the same soul, our journeys weren't the same. She had lessons to learn too. But the only reason we were brought together was to help each other learn these final few lessons of the soul. It spoke of enlightenment. And how usually the chaser was slightly more enlightened than the runner.

As I researched, I realized this was exactly what was happening, I began to think back at some the actions, of both her and the reactions of myself, I thought about the Fact that I "just know" at times. And it explained why we couldn't move on. In short it said that once 2 twins meet, things will never be the same. Before flames come together, Ignorance is bliss so to speak. But once the universe brings them together, the connection is recognized by the soul. And well, you can't UN-know something.

I read books that explained perfectly the initial unexplainable instant love and connection we both felt. Everything I read confirmed everything we had gone through was because we were in fact, Twin flames.

Chapter 16

Once I realized she had chosen to leave her home and move in with him, I didn't care anymore what the possible reason was. I had spent so much time making excuses for her already and I was exhausted. The last thing I told her (of course through text.) was that if she went through with this move. I would be gone forever. I was truly just defeated. I knew I loved her. I knew we were connected spiritually for a reason, and I was beginning to realize the truth about what we were and even some reasons why we have deteriorated to this, yet even with the other man involved, she couldn't let go any more than I could. Although she was much stronger in my view, and well...stubborn as a mule. But no matter what I believed, it really didn't matter if she didn't see it and understand it too. So to me, I was just wasting my time. And creating more heartache for myself. I decided that if I could manage to let go of her, then she wouldn't have a choice.

I dedicated myself to learning as much as I could about twin flames. In truth, I was searching for something that said everything would eventually come back to the way it was meant to be. But I didn't find that in any of the books.

Summer came and I hadn't spoke to her in months. I did however send her a simple text on her birthday saying "I hope you have a good day". To which she responded with "I'll try".

That was it. It seemed a bit off. And of course being able to feel her energy, I knew from those two words she wasn't happy. But I left it alone. And moved on. I had spent that summer preparing for my son to go away to college. For me that was going to be difficult. And I knew it. Me and the kids spent a good portion of the days on the pool deck with the rest of our family. I did my best to keep my mind occupied. I was determined to let her go. I was still researching energy and how it fits into the Twin flames scenario. And what to expect as time moved forward. I began to find information about what a chaser was. What a runner was. And what triggers each. I learned that there I generally a Masculine dominant energy, and a feminine dominant energy, but not to be confused because they are not necessarily assigned the man or woman twin flame. However it is most common for the female flame to be the chaser, and the Man to be the runner. In our case this was reversed. (I'll explain more in Part two).

But nothing I found really gave me any idea of what to do about any of this information. But one article did suggest I take a step back and examine what I'd learned. What major lessons I had learned or was learning throughout this journey. So I did that.

The first thing I learned was true forgiveness. What it is and how to give it to someone. For me that seemed like a lesson not to many people learn. Or even consider. But for me it was clear early on that I had to learn it. I believe this was at least part of my soul lessons.

The other thing I learned, but didn't realize, was the true meaning of unconditional love. A lot of people use this term but cannot actually fathom what it means. And through my studies I have come to believe, only True Twin Flames learn this.

Those are the 2 major lessons I can say I've learned throughout this journey. I will address them more later.

But even with a new understanding, and a new awakening. In my mind I couldn't put it all together, and make sense of one thing. What difference does it make if I understand everything? What would it matter if I learned all these lessons, if I was the only one of the two that understood? She was still running and doing her best to hide from the truth.

The effect of everything I had and was still learning was changing the way I looked at life. And Louise. Where once I was bitter and angry, asking "How could she do this to me". Now I see that she really didn't have a choice. I couldn't have learned these lessons if we had not separated. I believe I know the lessons she needs to address but I can't tell her. It's something she has to come to by herself. But the more awakened she becomes, the more clear her lessons become. And once reunion is achieved, together our soul energy is the strongest and we can help each other. But at this point, I just couldn't see any of that happening.

Chapter 17

It was July 28th. I didn't realize it at the time, but it was exactly one year to the day that she had left me. I had not communicated with the exception of the Birthday text, in a few months. No, I was not getting over her. I still prayed for her every day. And for some reason believed that she would find her way back to us. I loved her even more now than the day she left. My connection to her was still new to me, but learned to understand when I feeling something, to go with it.

It was the afternoon, late in my work day, something didn't feel right. I picked up the phone and checked her social media page. I found that she had posted a sort of cryptic message she had copied and pasted. I didn't know what it meant, something along the lines of relying on yourself and being your own happiness, or something to that effect. As I stated before, although it was unspoken, she knew I watched her page and knew what she posted, I would see.

Even though I hadn't communicated with her in months, and I hadn't actually seen her in a year, or even heard her voice, I decided to send her a text, and just ask if she was ok. So I did.

She responded with something to the effect of leaning, and lessons, and regrets.
I asked her what she was referring to. And the flood gates opened up. She responded with a message telling me all the things she wished she would have done differently with us. I was in a sort of shock. I never expected her to open up to me like that. And I had no idea what had triggered it.

She said she wished she hadn't tried to be so tough all the time. She wished she hadn't developed that pipe bomb, I'll show you attitude. She wished she would have just stopped sometimes and just loved me through whatever we were dealing with. And she said she wished she had never told me she didn't want to get married, because she does. But because she always had to be tough, she never let me know that.

As I said, after reading this text, I was dumbfounded. It had been a year of trashing me and lying to me and her moving in with another man, and running and hiding... but here it was. A little bit of truth, a little bit of acknowledgement.
I honestly could only think of one thing to say. "I'll marry you right now Louise"

Silence followed. She would respond telling me she was absolutely speechless. Had no words to respond to my message. After all this time and all she had put me through. As simple as that, she realized I never stopped loving her. Never lost faith in her. And I was the one person in this world she would always have.

It was an amazing moment. At that time I had always carried the ring I had bought for her but never got the chance to give. I pulled it out and took a picture of the ring on my pinky finger, and sent it. Along with the words "I mean it."

From there we opened up a bit of conversation. Really nothing to heavy. Mostly me, trying to get her to tell me what triggered this. She told me she felt as if she was drowning. She had begun to realize all the mistakes she had made in the last year. And the hole she had put herself in. She wanted to make everything right again but didn't know how.

I did my best to be supportive. Reassure her nothing was lost and that I still had faith in her even if she didn't have faith in herself.

Over the next week or two, we actually kept in contact. I was explaining some of the changes I had gone through, how I had come to these changes. I told her about the forgiveness. We discussed some of the old issues and I listened, and she talked, and then I both apologized and explained my side of the story. Calmly while she listened. This alone was amazing and enormous growth in and of itself. I also explained that who's right and who's wrong didn't matter to me anymore. And I can see the big picture in everything, which is something she should focus on. Not just what's in front of your face at the time. And most of the things we argued about were insignificant in the grand scheme.

I also talked to her about how nearly all of our problems stemmed from the same two things. Time and communication. In essence, we fought so much because we loved each other so much and only wanted more. The lack of communication was because we didn't understand that loving each other was the reason for the good and the bad.

I had repeatedly asked her to get together for lunch or to call at night, and each time she would have reason not to. Finally she said

"I live with another man, I can't just start seeing you or pick up the phone"

I responded with, "I did not know that"

She had never said she was moving in with him. I had told her if she did I was going to disappear. I assumed she had, but now she was contacting me. I guess I thought maybe I was wrong. But I wasn't.

She had told me she wanted to leave him and his house. Not because he wasn't a good guy but because she knew it was me she was meant to be with. I pushed for her to take action and do what she said, I wanted that so bad. She agreed that once she got the kids off to college she would be able to dedicate herself to coming up with a plan.

In the mean time I would have to just wait. I thought, what the hell right? I had waited this long. And now I was in a spot where I was something I never really wanted to be. The other man. And that wore on me. But in my mind I kept asking myself, was I really the other man, or was he? Amazing the way the mind can rationalize pretty much anything. Over the next week or so, we continued to communicate via text. I hated it. I hadn't even heard her voice in over a year. And so much gets lost in translation through email and text. I think she could tell I was not doing very well with being patient. And one day my phone rang.

I was sitting at my desk in my office, and the phone buzzed and I looked down and saw her face on the ID. My heart jumped, and I damn near broke the phone trying to answer it as fast as I could. When I finally said hello, I know my voice was shaky. I heard her say "Hi there" as she always did. And her voice I could tell was shaky as well, as we both did our best not to let the other know we were emotional. The sound of her voice was like an angel whispering. I have no other way to describe it. It was like an instant calm, and all was right in the world again.

We only spoke for a few minutes, and I made sure I spoke in very clear intentions so there was no misunderstanding. I asked her point blank if I was correct in my understanding that her intentions were to leave him and that town, and come back to us. She said YES. But she also stated that it wouldn't be easy, and I'd have to respect him throughout this as well. This did not make me happy. I asked her why I should care one bit about his or anyone else's respect, when they all knew what they were doing to me when they took you away. Where was my respect? I quite honestly told her to do what needed to be done, but do not ever ask me to respect the person who knowingly interfered with our relationship.

She agreed, and said she was going to speak to him when he got home. But as usual, this never happened. And more weeks went by with long periods of silence. She would promise to do something and never deliver. Never spoke to him about us or what she wanted, never took any steps to move toward us. Just a lot of talk. And at this point I was numb to it. The woman I had once trusted with my life, I would have taken a bullet for, now couldn't be counted on for a simple phone call. Or to follow through with anything.

Chapter 18

As all of this unfolded, I was given promises after promises, that she was Packing her stuff. That she would tell him the truth. But nothing ever happened. Then one day in September, she asked if we could meet somewhere and talk. She chose to meet at a town walking path, and go for a walk so we could talk. When I arrived I was nervous. I hadn't laid eyes on her in well over a year. And to be honest I wasn't sure she would even show up. But as I saw her pull her truck up and park it next to mine, I felt the tears starting to come. Tears of fear, tears of joy, of regret, I wasn't sure. But I got out of the truck and walked around as she did the same. When she came into view only a few feet away, I actually hesitated to even look at her. I guess I was afraid this moment wasn't real. But when I lifted my head and looked into her eyes I could see that smile on her face. And we were drawn together again.

I didn't have a clue what to expect from this, so I was a bit standoffish. I immediately hugged her as I always did every time we came together. But quickly let go and stepped back. We started walking down the path, and we hadn't gone 100 yards and she had begun telling me how difficult this would be for her to do, and how good of a guy he was, so she had to be respectful, etc. I stopped dead in my tracks and asked her. "Louise, do you love me or not"

She responded, "Yes I love you, I have always loved you, it never stopped."

As we walked some more, she explained that she couldn't leave his house right now because he had been arrested for a DWI. And consequently had his driver's license revoked. Because of this, she had to drive him back and forth to his work locations so he didn't lose his job. She said she felt she owed it to him to help him, and this was only a 30 day issue. After that he would be able to get his license back.

I asked her why I should care one bit about what his problems were. I knew a few things about the man already, and he wasn't the saint that Louise was trying to portray. She knew it and I knew it. But what choice did I have. I couldn't force her to do anything.

As we walked we talked about how she was going to leave. And what she would do when all her new friends she had that were his family, turned on her. She didn't seem worried, in fact, her words were "They will just have to deal with it won't they."

As we returned to the trucks, I asked her what now? I'm just supposed to sit and wait. I suggested that given what was coming, her leaving him, Perhaps she should prepare herself by removing her profiles from social media for a while. That way people can't use that platform to attack her. She agreed. We also agreed that just because she felt she owed something to him, that the end result was inevitable. And there was no reason we couldn't continue to communicate, and rebuild us. She agreed. But I also made it clear, that from here on out, her word needs to be golden. I need to be able to count on you to deliver the things you say you will. And she understood and agreed. She tried to reassure me by telling me that whatever this was between us clearly isn't going away, so she wants to put right her mistakes so we can move on.

As she left I grabbed her and kissed her. I honestly didn't think about it. It's just what I always did. But when her lips touched mine I realized I maybe should have asked first. But when I pulled away, I could see the love in her eyes, even if she was trying to hide it. I could see the smile, she did her best to conceal. I asked if she wanted to just plan on meeting there again next week at the same time. She agreed and was on her way.

As the week went on, we communicated through text again. Nothing dramatic, mostly me pushing her to do what she had said. To make plans and begin her move. He worked out of town all week so to me, she should be moving her stuff during the week. At least the things in the shed and the things she didn't need every day. She claimed she was, but she wasn't. She was doing the bare minimum. Which was nothing.

When the following Friday came and we were supposed to meet again, she had to cancel for some reason, I expected, here we go again, but to my surprise she just moved the meeting to Saturday.

When Saturday arrived she showed up, in his Truck. Not hers. Kind of insulting I thought, but she had said that her daughter was driving hers. And her other guy just told her to take his and don't hurry home. Obviously she didn't tell him where she was headed.

We walked a bit in a park, and talked about what was happening. She told me the 30 day issue with his license was over. She said she had to take him to a meeting with the lawyer and the judge the previous day and that's why she had to cancel. I was happy. Not only hadn't she blown me off, but now the obstacle in her way was removed. And she could begin whatever her plan was to leave him. She was clearly a bit nervous about this, and I did everything possible to encourage her and empower her to just bite the bullet and get it done. If he was such a good guy as she had previously claimed then he would be happy for her. (I knew otherwise).

When we parted, I kissed her, and she drove away. Clearly nervous about what she had just told me she knew she had to do. She texted me about an hour later. Said she was glad to be able to see me again, and wanted me to know that I was right. And she planned on speaking with him that evening. I said ok. Contact me when it's done.

As evening turned into night, I hadn't heard from her. I texted her and she eventually responded, and told me that she was still talking to him. I was at least happy to hear she was doing what she said she would. But that was the last I'd hear from her that night. The next day I tried to get out of her how it had went and is it done. She only responded that they still had things to talk about. As soon as she told me this, I knew it wasn't going to happen. Even though she claimed he was supportive and asked what she needed from him. But as time went on it became clear that that wasn't the truth. She might have spoken to him, or intended to, but she never told him anything about me, or us, or her plan to leave. I just shook my head and left it alone. I couldn't believe that the lady I once could count on, was now … well this.

About a week went by and she sent me pictures of her home in Shinglehouse. There had been a water line break, and the house had been soaked for days, or longer. Since no one lived there at the time the water could have been running for a week. Her kitchen cabinets had fallen off the wall from all the water damage. The basement had flooded and destroyed her heating systems. The leak had originated from the second floor bathroom, so everything was destroyed. The insurance adjuster would set the damages at approximately $70,000.

I knew this was going to be the new reason she wasn't going to leave him and the house she currently was living in with him. I tried to get out ahead, knowing what was coming. I somehow convinced her to come to my house and visit. And to my surprise she did. As we talked I told her she and her daughter were more than welcome to come stay with me, while her home was being rebuilt. I offered to buy her daughter a new car so she could drive herself to school so she wouldn't have to change districts. But of course none of these offers were accepted. And as I knew was going to happen. This was the new reason she now had to not move and follow through with her supposed plan.

Dealing with insurance took a while. But once the construction began, it went even slower. She had hired a contractor who worked alone, and would spend hours at her house. He would stay until 9:00 pm some nights. And when I asked Louise why he wasn't getting anything done, she always had an excuse. I didn't understand this since she said she was going over to the house after work to help. Then it hit me. This contractor was staying late on purpose to try and hit on her. I brought this up to Louise and of course she told me how wrong I was. I pointed out that for all the time he was spending there, nothing was getting done. Why might that be? Again she told me how wrong I was. And now I told her I not only had to deal with the man she was living with, but I had to worry about the contractor who she was spending hours with every night. It was later that she would tell me she wasn't going over after work anymore. Apparently he had made a move on her of some sort and according to her, she had to be very blunt and slam the door closed so to speak. That was as close as I'll ever get to being told I was right. But it did nothing for our situation. A job that should have taken 2 months for one man full time, took him a year. And I don't believe Louise really cared, because as long as the house wasn't done, she would always have an excuse not to leave the other guy.

She offered to move into the second floor of her business. But then that never happened. She said the contractor was finishing the second floor bathroom and her bedroom first, so she could live there and lock the door. But of course that never happened either. She said she would rent a place in town until it was done. You guessed it, never happened.

It became clear to me that she was never going to move. What wasn't clear to me is why was she stringing me along then? I figured out very early that she was using this man for one reason. He had a home in the school district her daughter wanted to be in. Louise was incapable of telling her children no. Or standing up for what she wanted when it came to her children. And the situation with her daughter was even worse. Not because of her daughter. But because she was the youngest and the last. I don't believe her daughter ever realized that her mother was in effect using her as a reason not to have to commit to us. As I always said, Louise was taking the easiest road possible. And yes she wished she had done things differently, but facing the reality of what it was going to take to make them right, was just too overwhelming for her. So instead of trying and doing something difficult to get what she really wanted, she decided not to. And to settle and take the easy route. Something she would later admit. The ease of the life she has, vs, the challenge of the life she really wants.

Chapter 19

Throughout all of this, I was pushing. In my mind, she had a year of hell she put me through. And I was happy she understood that. But here we were, almost another year gone, and nothing had changed. The only difference was now she talked to me. Now she told me lies, and refused to follow through with anything she said. I told her on more than one occasion, that her words mean nothing. I began to realize that all this was doing was making it easier for me to just turn my back and walk away. Flame or no flame. What did it matter if I would have to waste my life? And this was now year number 6. What good were the lessons and answers I had attained, if I would never get to put them to use. So I pushed. The more she lied and hid the more I pushed. And where I had gotten past the bitterness and anger, it was now creeping back. I felt like she was toying with me. Just because she could. And because of this I pushed even more. And no more was I tiptoeing around her in fear of pissing her off. When she would tell me she would do something, I made other plans anyway, because she was so predictable. And when she left me hanging, I'd call her a liar. When she claimed she loved me I would simply say prove it. I was over all the crap being thrown at me. There was no way god or the universe would punish one man like this for so long. Finding my Twin flame was no blessing, it was a curse. For both of us. All the power and decisions concerning the future of both of our lives resided with a woman that wasn't strong enough to even stand up for us to her own children. Let alone her friends and family. And what about the other man. He was being lied to as well. And the longer this went on the worse it was going to be for all involved. So I pushed, for some sort of ending. Some sort of closure. I had hoped she would grow to see what was happening, but she never did.

The holidays approached once more. And of course I was anxious. I knew this situation wasn't going to be solved before. I knew I was going to be the one left out. I pushed her to finally tell him the truth. And for the 3rd or 4th time she said she would. And for the 3rd or 4th time she didn't. Christmas came and went. And after Christmas she said she had to attend a late family Christmas at her mothers. I was familiar with this because it's the same as I used to attend with her. Only later would I find out, she took him with her.

I was so embarrassed, and jealous at the same time. What the Hell was this woman doing? She had to be screwing with my head on purpose. Either she had just been caught lying to me again. And had never said a word to him. Or they were both lying to everyone, including her family pretending to be the happy couple. Which was no different than spitting in my face.

A few months earlier I had given Louise the Engagement ring I had bought her, and asked her to marry me. Not today, but someday. And she said yes. And was wearing the ring. But how could she wear the ring and still pretend everything was alright with him? I was at my breaking point. I told her that either she was going to tell him the truth once and for all, or I would. She didn't even flinch. Her response was go ahead, she didn't care if I did it. Obviously she never thought I would. Boy was she wrong.

I was so pissed that not only could she toy with me and lie to me and take every ounce of effort that I had to offer and then spit in my face, but then she would go home at night to another man. And to top that off, she had somehow managed to make me live with it and keep me strung along all this time. Not any more,

I pulled up Facebook and looked his profile up. I sent him a private message telling him I didn't understand how he could still live with a woman that was engaged to another man. And if he didn't believe me, just look at the ring on her finger.

I also sent the same message to His daughter. She was fresh out of high school and hated Louise. I was sending it to her because I knew exactly how Louise would handle him. She would lie, cry, and manipulate him when backed into a corner. But She couldn't manipulate the people outside the house that loved him, and if they too knew the truth. It would end.

But in my state of mind, I really didn't care what the effect on OUR relationship was. The bitterness had reemerged. How dare she treat me this way?

I was reminded of a counseling session in which Kate said multiple times...

"you can lead a horse to water, but what do you do when you can't make it drink?"

Well, Guess what? The answer is ... You shoot the horse.

The only way to ensure the horse doesn't suffer anymore is to put it out of its misery. If you don't, it is assured a long slow painful death.

That's what I did. I told the other man just enough to make him ask Louise and make her try to either do what was right, or squirm. But in the process, the truth was going to come out one way or another.

The message sent to the other man was received. And I know this because all hell broke loose at approx. 5:00am. One morning. He responded to the message asking who I was. (I had used a dummy name because if I didn't he wouldn't have taken it seriously) I never responded.

Shortly after that Louise began texting me and calling me every name in the book. Actually telling me how I didn't care if I fucked her life up blah blah. Just a ton of the nastiest thing you'd ever hear. I told her I didn't understand why she was mad, I told her I was going to do it, and she said ok, go ahead. (a mistake she will never make again). Her response was that since I stirred the shit, I was going to have to lick the spoon till it all settled. I said no. I wouldn't be doing that.

The message to his daughter was never received. I look back at this as divine intervention, because that would have been the final dagger. She would have caused so much trouble that Louise's pride would never allow her to come back to us. This at the time was the plan. To piss her off and make her feel a sliver of my humiliation and hurt. Knowing she would never return from it. So I could finally move on with my life. It was, and attempt to shoot the horse.

Chapter 20

As I said before, I was pushing the whole way. To me there was no reason to not step up and do the right thing, once you know you made a mistake and wanted it to be fixed. I knew all along it was nothing but one stall tactic after another. She has used, Her mother, Her daughter numerous times, Her sons, Her job, Her house, Hell even her dog, cat, and her live in man's dog, all as excuses. And the more she hid behind the most obvious things, the more I pushed. I wanted to take away all of her excuses until she had none and had to finally start telling the truth.

But the more I pushed the more she ran, the more ridiculous the reasoning became. She would contradict herself all the time. But what I didn't realize, was this was a cycle. It didn't matter which came first. The chicken or the egg. Didn't matter if she ran so I chased. Or I chased so she ran. None of that mattered. The only thing that did matter was, the only way at this point that something good was going to come of this was for one of us to stop. And to this point I knew she was the runner. And I had an idea of what that meant for her and her actions. But believe it or not, I didn't stop and grasp what being the chaser meant to the situation. And how my actions in effect caused her reaction to run. Every bit as much as her running caused my reaction to chase. Hopefully that's not to confusing.

In fact a case could be made that by the simple act of chasing, and my own justifications for doing so, I was in theory running also. Running from facing my fears and unresolved issues. How's that for confusing?

In short, I was as much to blame for this as she was. To an outsider who has no idea about the concept of flames, this makes no sense. It's always some ones fault. And it just needed to end. But when you are in a twin flam relationship, ending is really not an option. But it does need to stop.

After the horse was shot, or so I thought, I left it alone. Stayed quiet and waited for words from her. This didn't last very long. Somehow after she calmed down she understood why I had done what I had done. And although she wasn't happy, and it caused a shit storm for her, she couldn't be mad at me for it.

Time went on and I was basically just on auto pilot. Nothing changed at all. I have no idea what she said to her other guy. But nothing changed. She still lived there, and she still would tell me she would do this or that and never follow through, she would say she would call and ghost me. All the same as usual.

The summer of 2019 came and went. All the same. At this point I was just spent. I had no more energy to give. I hated myself for not being able to just go find a new love. It was impossible. Over the past 2 years I had been drinking more. Of course I was, I had no one at all to talk to except Kate, and even then I felt as if my only friend was only my friend because I paid her to be. I was in constant misery, and stress. I drank after work every day and I justified it by saying I can't sleep if I don't. My mind won't shut off. By this time I even began to ask myself why in the world Louise would bother coming back. Every time she let me down I blew up. Said some things that weren't necessary. And I would feel disgusted with myself, and I would send her my apologies. And every time she would assure me that she understood how I felt. But it didn't make it any easier. I was becoming someone I never wanted to be. In essence, I was losing who I am, in my pursuit of her and us.

Back in march I had dropped a box off for her at her house, now fully rehabbed, and ready to be lived in. there were no more excuses, yet she wasn't living there. Her daughter now had her own car. And her father lived in the same town as her school. The other man's house was no longer necessary or a road block, yet she was still there.

In the box was a bunch of gifts I had bought for her over time. Included were several books about the twin flame theory. As I said that was in March.

To date, I have not seen her since then. Summer came and went. More of the same. I had 2 tickets for us to go to our beach in Florida for a long weekend for my birthday in September. This wasn't just me being optimistic, she had told me she wanted to go. But as is the normal now, as time grew closer, she began back peddling. I simply told her one week before we were scheduled to leave, that if she went, we would use the time to remind each other how and why we love each other in the first place. We would use the uninterrupted time to have fun together, and recharge each other and it would be our new beginning. No looking back. But if she did not go, then I was done. I believe she figured I wasn't serious, because I had said that so many times and still I was right there every time she reached. But whether she understood it or not. I was done. I was giving up. I knew I would always love her. There would never be anyone else, but I was surrendering. She wins. Run if you want but I'm not chasing you anymore. Come get what you claim you want or stay in the life you admit you don't want. The struggle is over.

The difference this time is simple. My heart just couldn't take the beating anymore. I had nothing to have faith in anymore. And she went out of her way to cause me pain and suffering at every effort. I was humiliated for who I had become. I didn't even like myself anymore. I had neglected so much of my life over the past 2 + years, and it was time to give up the fight and get my life back. Only a fool keeps doing the same thing over and over expecting a different result.

The very second I truly surrendered, not just words, but truly surrendered, it was not a conversation with her. It just was. And in that moment, she felt the energy I had given and directed to her for years, leave her.
She was in the doctor's office waiting in the waiting room, and had brought one of the books I had given her. She just opened it up to a random page and began to read. What she was reading was a description of a runner. And the ways they do the most despicable, mean and cruel things to their chaser, there one true love.

In an instant she knew. She had that lightbulb, ah ha, I get it now moment. She was so amazed at how the book described her to a "T". It had finally clicked. She was awake.

She hadn't spoke to me in a few days, and she took out her phone and snapped a picture of the page and sent it to me. Asking if I had read this. I told her of course I had read all the books I had given her. She was so amazed at how it perfectly described us, she went back and read the book from the beginning. And when that one was done, she read the next one. And the next one. I was happy for her, and she was excited, to be gaining this knowledge. She couldn't get enough. I still was basically silent. I had heard her wonderful promises before only to be let down. A few days later she told me she would not be going with me on the trip. And for me that was it. She said she wanted to learn more and as the reading said face her fears that have held her back. And while I think that's wonderful for her. It changed nothing for me. I told her she cannot change anything until she leaves her safety net which is the other man. She may identify fears, but she will never truly conquer them until she commits to it. And I told her, because of all the hell she put me through, I wouldn't believe her to be serious until she cut the cord with the other man. You can't have your cake and eat it too. Can't be half way committed to two different people. And as much as I believed in her as my twin. I would never put myself through this hell again. I will never accept a relationship with a woman who has one foot out the door already. And my biggest fear is that all I have done is give her a new excuse to use to stall. I have believed for a long time that she was doing her best to just ride this out as long as she could with the goal of never leaving him until her daughter is out of school and he and his home is no longer needed. If that comes true, she will have been inflicting pain and hell on me for over 2 years. And what's worse, I knew exactly what she was doing and I thought I could change it.

Chapter 21

As of the date of this writing, she has yet to actually do anything. She says she is doing the work, taking notes reading books researching etc. But I have seen nothing being done. The few times she has contacted me, I have responded with the fact that I really don't care what she is doing. None of it matters until she proves it. And she can't do that without leaving him. Nothing else matters to me until she does.

She has shared one of her fears, and of course the solution is not hard to see. It's easy to write down a fancy paragraph about a fear you have, but it makes no difference at all if you aren't committed to overcoming it.
I have hopes i guess, but not many. IT has been so long and I've struggled and scratched and clawed for us, only to be rejected at every turn. Every time I thought, maybe this time, I was let down and left heartbroken yet again.

I still believe with all my heart that we are twin flames and this was meant to be. The problem I'm having, is being happy about it. After getting beat down for so long, no matter if I understand why, it still takes a toll. And I think the one thing to remember is that we are human. No matter the books you read, or what they say, we as humans can only carry so much. And unfortunately I am beginning to feel as if I have had enough. People make this twin flame thing out to be the most miraculous and wonderful thing in the universe. From where I sit, it's nothing but pain and suffering, and hurt, inflicted by the one you love more than anything.

We all have a role to play. Understanding is key to survival of this twin flame thing. But even then, nothing guarantees success. There is no guarantee that you won't wake up and realized you wasted 30 yrs.' of your life waiting on you twin to finally get it, but they never do. Then what?

In closing this section, I want to say, Good luck. It will be a long and difficult road. The runner will do some amazingly difficult things to the chaser, and the chaser will continue to push. It is going to be painful for the both of you. But I also believe everything in your life leading to now has prepared you to handle this last lesson.

Thank you for reading, as I said I know I'm not a great author. I hope I explained well enough that in part two we can follow the timeline of what the books say in comparison to our situation. Thank you. Part 2 coming up.

Part 2

Chapter 1

As we roll back the pages and revisit the story you just read, I will try to show some of the similarities in our story to some of the other books out there on the market. I will also attempt to show you that even though Louise did and said some pretty amazingly insulting things, that there was indeed a reason for it. And at time she had no choice.

I will point out the importance of what exactly a chaser does, and How chasing has no positive effect on the future of the relationship. Yet even knowing that, means nothing. It is just something you cannot stop doing until it's time to surrender.

I will do my best to explain the Energy shared between the two flames and how it affects each. Of course I am an ordinary man and not a professor, so I'll do my best to explain, in the same way I learned, Laymen's terms that everyone can understand.

And of course the stages that others have written about, and where I and Louise are now, I think.

One more thing before we get started with part 2. I know that in the first part of this book, my descriptions of what was happening, portrayed Louise and being in essence a cold hearted bitch. I hope you will see that this wasn't necessarily her fault. And that I played my role in making it that way. I wrote this from the Chaser perspective that I had throughout this journey. And as of this writing, I cannot get her perspective to share her side, which clearly would make things a little less lop sided.

Despite anything written I wish to make clear I do understand her role. I do understand what not only made her run, but what made her keep running. And remember, just because they piss you off doesn't mean you don't love them. It just means they pissed you off. And while she was a pro at pissing me off, I still to this day love her with all that I am. And whether there is a reunion or not, she will always be my twin flame.

Chapter 2

When I began this book, I gave some background on both of us, briefly. I did that because I believe that every hardship each of us has endured prior to meeting, was meant to prepare us in the best possible way, to be successful at navigating these difficult times that came after meeting.

Separations of twin flames is perhaps the hardest thing in the world for a soul to overcome. So it stands to reason that the hardships of poverty, being single parents, Previous failed relationships and the heartache that came with them, all were necessary and probably preordained by us before birth. Necessary to teach us the necessary life and soul lessons to build our strength so that we may have a fighting chance. Perseverance is key.

As most of you already know, the initial love and attraction, in every way, between two flames is undeniable and unexplainable. It is so strong it is truly scary. Why do I say scary? Simple, Scared of losing it. Scared of it not being real. Always waiting for the other shoe to drop. Scared of being hurt again as we had in our past. Scared of making a mistake and screwing it up, as some have in the past. And the list goes on and on. These fears may be the same for a lot of normal relationships, but the fears develop over time. For Twins they are instant. As they were with me. Remember when I wrote about feeling not good enough after our first date? It wasn't Louise's fault. She didn't do anything to make me feel I wasn't good enough. It was me. It was partly because of past scars from previous relationships, but mostly because the intensity of the attraction from day one was just multiplied exponentially after physically being in the same place. The joint energies made us both a sort of euphoric. Twin flames are 2 halves of the same source. Separately we had evolved and grown into very strong individuals. But together, we were truly one. Neither of us knew that at the time though. So when we separated, we went from that euphoria type feeling, back to only half of that. And the way that affected me was to see everything in my life that I did not perceive to be good enough for her. Louise on the other hand had a different effect. Cautious optimism. She was a very cautious person at that time and very guarded, no doubt due to her past experiences, and scars. Her fears were about why she felt it difficult to be guarded when we were together.

Looking back, I needed her walls down to real me in from my embarrassment of what I thought would drive her away. And she need to see me humbled and have to face making the choice, telling the embarrassing truth to save us, or choosing not to and just walking away and being like every other man she had known.

While it sounds bad for a first issue right out of the gate, it was exactly how it was supposed to be. I showed her immediately that I wasn't just a bunch of words, and showed her immediately that I was more concerned with her than myself.

And she showed me not all women are the same. Something that sounds simple enough, but that I had put a wall around. She wouldn't be denied, which is why she reached out in the first place. And she showed me what it was like to stand behind someone regardless of their living, financial, social, whatever...situation.

We had no idea what the reasoning was or that it was this profound at the time. We only knew we had some unexplainable reason why we were so drawn to each other.

From this point on we entered what was described by most other authors as the "bubble love" phase. No, I don't have a damn clue who came up with that term, but it is what it is right?

Everything was beyond perfect. More than either of us ever imagined. We talked very early on about marriage and living together. The only reason this wasn't possible was because of the necessary living arrangements for the kids, hers and mine. So we knew going in that it was going to be difficult and likely a long time before we would be free to pursue those options.

We would talk, and discover how close we actually came on several occasions throughout our lives, to coming together. The college she had followed her brother and then boyfriend, to, was the same school I attended. And it was only a matter of months that we missed each other by. She knew some of the same people I had met, and I probably had met her brother and her then boyfriend during my time there. After this, we were talking about a concert we had both been at, and yet again, just missed each other.

Years later, while building her business, she would visit the Home Depot often with her then business partner, who was well aware of the troubles in Louises relationship, and was pushing her to meet someone new. Her partner would suggest she meet the manager of the store. She didn't, but ironically, the manager of the store was a good friend of mine. And I too was then working there. We found out later that her Long time best friend was pushing her to meet a good friend. Louise never agreed, but as it turns out, that friend is the man that is now my IT guy at my office.

Time and time again, the universe kept us close. As we started realizing how close we came on so many different occasions to meeting, we began to see that this wasn't really normal. Keep in mind, we didn't live right down the road from each other. We were over an hour apart. And when you think about the instant and amazing connection that was our relationship, it begins to become clear that the universe WANTED us to be together.

But this where the idea of "Divine timing" comes in to play. Had we actually met on any of those other occasions, the timing wouldn't have been right and we would most likely have missed our chance. Twin Flames, once brought together cannot ever really be separated. And if the universe had allowed us to be brought together before we were ready, we wouldn't have had the life experiences we had to have to prepare us for it.

At first, at least for me, the more synchronicities that appeared, the more confirmation it gave that yes this was in fact a god given opportunity. Exciting and heartwarming, but also scary as hell. There was no, letting go. No, walking away. Sure, at that point everything was wonderful, but what happens when the relationship was tested? Just because we had found each other, didn't mean there still wasn't everyday life to contend with. The human emotions, of Love, Jealousy, outside interference. And once I began to understand how rare a relationship like ours was, the more of a sort of pressure I felt to not screw it up.

Chapter 3

The "Bubble Love" phase for us was absolutely amazing. The love we each felt from each other was like nothing either of us had ever experienced. It wasn't just passion and joy, but for me it was instantly like I had found my best friend. And to be madly in love with your best friend, is in its self a whole other level. She would meet me at the door every time I arrived. I couldn't walk past her at any point, or allow her to walk past without reaching for her. Just to touch her. It was an involuntary thing. Just automatic. I would wrap her in my arms several times a day. No matter who was around. And through everything, from day one till the day she left me, that never changed. Every time I saw her every day, I told her how beautiful she was, and how much I loved her. From start to finish.

She would drive to my crappy run down trailer, while I was at work and the kids were in school, and bring a crock pot, and cook dinner and it would be waiting when me and the kids got home. She would come, prepare it and then leave to go back and take care of her own kids. She did this more than once. And each time it would bring tears to my eyes. I had never had a woman go out of their way like that, not for me. It was actually hard to know how to respond. What words to use to express my appreciation?

She would go grocery shopping for her home, and come back with not only groceries for her family, but she would see things she thought I might like or the kids would like and buy bags and bags of groceries for me to. It was really the most selfless act I had ever had a woman give. In the Early stages I stated, I was embarrassed about the living situation I was in. I was at that time building a house for the kids and I, because I thought it was the only way I was ever going to be able to give them something better. I had secured the land through a family friend. And began construction a couple of years before I met Louise. Yes, I said a couple of years. Where I live at least, securing a mortgage to build a home was difficult. 20 percent down minimum, Excellent credit requirements, difficult to get the finance company to let me build it myself.

And I already knew that after the divorce, and the bankruptcy, I couldn't get qualified for a conventional mortgage. So I began building a little at a time. Whenever I had a few extra dollars that is where it would go. Lumber, and material for the new house. The problem was I didn't have much money. So the actual construction was going extremely slow. And my children were at that time too young to actually help with much. So every nail driven, was by my hand. Every board cut was by my hand.

Louise always said she loved it up there. Where the house was located was up in the woods. Off an old seasonal dirt road. She also enjoyed working with her hands, and so for a while she would go up and try to help as much as she could. Or she would bring me lunch when I was up there working. But most of the time, it wasn't labor I needed, it was material. I really never had much more than enough material for about a half of a day's work. And then I'd have to wait until I could save for some more. She was supportive. Even offering to help buy materials on occasion.

The problems started, when I was faced with unanticipated dilemma. I worked a full time job Monday through Friday. And then the kids would go to their mothers for the weekend. Which left me with the choice of, going to see Louise and spending that time that we both cherished together, or spending time up on the property working on the new house. And then of course there was always the normal everyday things at the trailer I had to get done. Like cleaning (which I admit was a weakness), mowing the lawn, Laundry, shopping, etc.

Louise on the other hand ran her own business. And was successful enough that she only worked 2 to 3 days a week and only for about 4 hours at a time. She had all the time in the world to get hose same house hold obligations done during the week. I did not. I had Saturday, and Sunday. I don't think she ever really understood this. And in hindsight I believe this is where the problems started.

She had without a doubt been the perfect, loving partner. I adored her more than I ever expressed. And I was wrong for not doing more to show her. The problem was I didn't know how. Our lives were in very different places at the time. She felt that she was giving all of herself to the relationship, which she was. But she also felt that I was not giving back to her the same effort. She wanted more time. As did i. But there just wasn't enough time in the day or days in the week.

And not just that. I was giving everything I had. The difference that most people don't see, is that it's all relevant. One person's best might be a lot more than another person's. But it doesn't mean both aren't giving equally of themselves. Make sense?

If there's a homeless person somewhere, and a millionaire gives this homeless person $100. And another man gives him everything he has, but its only $50. Who actually gave more? No, it's not a math question.

So that's basically what was happening. She had gotten to a point in her life where she could do all these wonderful things for the relationship. And they were truly wonderful. She had all the time in the world as a product of her hard work paying off. And I was proud of her for that. But I did not.

She would tell me all the time how upset she would get when I would leave her house on a Sunday morning, because I had to go work on the house, or clean the trailer or shop before the kids got home, or whatever. She never really heard all this. She only saw me leaving at 10:00 am instead of spending that day together.

I understood. But I didn't know what choice I had. So the choice I made was to not work on the house as much. And a result of that decision was, I had more time with her. But the house would sit even longer with no progress. It was a conscious choice I made knowing the consequences. But she was right. We needed more time. And this was all I could do to give that to us. But as I started spending more time at her house, and staying later on Sundays, it was as if, nothing changed. She didn't even seem to notice the effort. And that bothered me. It was like she went straight from that issue to another one. Now all of the sudden I wasn't a very good house keeper, and that was a problem, and the reason she didn't give the effort to come to my house the same as I gave the effort to drive to her. Now don't get me wrong, I did suck at the domestic thing. I'm a nice guy, but I'm still a guy. But it was the same when she first met me. But now it was an issue where it wasn't before. So I made efforts to do a better job. But again.

Nothing changed. She just moved on to the next issue she found. This time it was the fact that I smoked. And I have to give it to her on this one, it is not a glamorous habit, and if you are not a smoker you know what I mean. But again, it wasn't as if I just started. I smoked when she met me. And I did promise her that I would never stop trying to quit. And to date, I still haven't accomplished it. But now it was a problem. So, I tried harder. Got different medications, to help, and could at times even manage to go for a couple days without it. Certainly a whole lot better than before. But it never mattered. Efforts were ignored and it was on to the next issue.

And this was the way things started to go. No more were there wonderful surprise dinners waiting for me. No more were there examples of her going out of her way to do those amazing things for us. And the reason was that she didn't feel I was giving all I had as she was. So she stopped.

Now. Looking at this situation, the actions are what stopped. She still loved me more than ever. But I think due to her past issues, she had in her mind that I was taking advantage of her kindness. As all of her ex's did. And that because she perceived she was doing and giving more to the relationship, I just automatically was holding back. I wasn't. I had no more to give. I did what I could. I did give all I had. I just didn't have that much to give. A concept she never really understood. Now that not to blame her for all the issues that ensued. I wasn't exactly easy. I worked a very high stress job and was barely making ends meet, on top of the stress any single parent feels. So to say I was distant at times or tense would be an accurate statement. But what she didn't realize was, all that tension and stress went away in an instant every time I looked at her. She would later tell me it wasn't until after she left me that she understood what that "look" I always gave her when I would see her after a week, meant. She always just wrote it off as me being a grump. But one day out of nowhere she thought about it and realized that wasn't it at all. That "Look" was one of relief. Finally we are together. "Ahhhh...ok everything's ok again, she's here".

It wasn't until the separation that she realized how lucky she really was. And how lucky WE were. It wasn't until the separation that she began to see some things from a different perspective. And understand why I said somethings I said. And did some things I did. Not everything of course, because not everything I did was right. And it was after she left that I began to understand so much more about how she felt. And why she felt it. I understood better why she wanted more time. It was just love. I understood why she was upset with me when I didn't give her the things she needed. And she now understood why it was I was unable to give her certain things. All things that were learned after the separation. And never would they have been understood if we had never separated, by either of us. Egos are a bitch. And very dangerous. And sometimes you have to step back and just see the big picture. And in that picture, does it really matter if she admits she's wrong? No it does not. Would it have been so bad to try a little harder to communicate or make a little more "us" time? No it wouldn't have. But in the moment, two strong willed people cannot put aside what there whole life has taught them. BE STRONG. DON'T SHOW WEAKNESS. NEVER BACK DOWN. These are what both of our lives leading up to this have taught us. We have had to have these mentalities and attitudes in order to survive the trials and tribulations of life so far. Which ironically, were meant to prepare us to be strong enough to handle the pain and difficulty of this Twin Flame reunion. Damn, hope you followed all that.

Chapter 4

I am a firm believer that when you are on the path, life is just easier. Things seem to fall into place for you when you need them to, in order to help you along the way. But when you stray from the path, your guides and the universe will attempt to steer you back. When your ego, or pride get in the way, and you won't pay attention to the signs given, sometimes the universe will punch you in the mouth to get your attention.

When Louise and I met, she had recently taken a severance package and was downsized at her job. She had been playing around with her own craft business for some time, with a coworker. So she used her severance and cashed out her 401K plan, to live on while she built this business full time. When we met she was making about $500 a week. And subsidizing her budget when necessary with her savings. She used to carry around a roll of cash that was very substantial, and keep it under the floor mat of her car. It used to drive me nuts when she would pull that thing out for some reason. I thought she was crazy to be carrying all that around with her. But I think it made her feel more secure to know it was with her.

A few months after we started dating, life not only was tremendously better for me. Obviously the infusion of this amazing all-encompassing love, but also through the wonderful acts Louise did for me, and my kids, she was showing me what love was meant to be. What it should be. For the first time in my life I believed there was more to life than just the everyday grind and struggle. No, I don't mean she was handing me over a ton of her hard earned money, although she offered on occasion and did help with certain things. It was truly the act. The kindness, and knowing that everything she did was truly out of love. In retrospect I think even she was amazed at how it felt to be on her end of it, and the love and joy we brought each other. She saw what it was like to have someone, that even though I was not as financially secure as she was, or live in a big house like she did, or even have nice things for that matter, none of it was taken for granted. Everything she did for me was so greatly appreciated, and never expected of her. It was as new for her as it was for me.

A few months in, her business started to really take off. She had hit on that hot new product that sent her sales through the roof. This was a welcome surprise. And more and more I would go to her house and do my best to help her out with production. And I loved every minute of it. I was so proud of her, and all of her accomplishments. And also it was a small way for me to give back some of the effort that she had already given. But to be honest I didn't even think of it in that way. I just loved being in some small way, a happy part of her life.

As the business grew, expansion was inevitable. Her and her business partner decided to build a "shed". That shed turned into the size of a small house. And rather than hire it to be built, we built it together. Right there in her front yard. And when the "shed" was almost complete, they also bought the house next door to run their operation out of, and used the shed for their equipment and building production.

Things were going amazingly well for her. Easy I guess you'd say. I viewed this as sign of being right on track in life. Her income more than tripled, her work hours were cut in half.

And for me, my work was picking up as well. I started getting raises. And because of this gained a bit of breathing room financially. I began taking Louise on week long vacations every year for her birthday. Why? Because I could. I wanted so badly to make her smile. That really was all there was to it. I loved our time together, and time was always an issue for us. So those trips were worth their weight in gold. And I admit. I knew the history of her past relationships. I knew none of them ever went above and beyond like that for her. So I was proud to be able to be the one to do that. The giving your best to us, that I spoke of in the previous chapter, was now getting more even. Life should have been wonderful for us. But I found that the more I was able to give her, the more she pushed back. As if, she didn't know how to react to someone showing her that kind of love and commitment. I was giving what she asked for, yet it wasn't making her any happier. In fact she fought me on most everything I ever tried to do for her. After returning from one of our trips to the beach, I had a letter in the mail, from a finance company. Basically it stated that I was approved for a mortgage. I hadn't even been thinking of buying, since I had the house still under construction. But I had all but stopped working on it. And it would take until the kids were long out of school to finish at this pace.

I went to her house one Friday, and as we sat on the back porch, I showed it to her and asked what she thought. She encouraged me to check it out and see what my options were. After making a few phone calls, and about 10 minutes, I was told that I was preapproved for a very large mortgage. I was excited to say the least. I had never bought a home before. The one with my ex-wife was hers. And here was a chance to get me and the kids out of that shit hole trailer that I wasn't even sure was going to last through another winter. But somehow, Louise didn't seem that happy for me. I tried hard to get her to look with me at homes, but all she would say is, "you have to live there, not me".

I wasn't quite sure why she never really was happy about it. The troubles between us had grown. And there were now outside influences chirping in her ear. I'm sure influences that wanted her away from me and were encouraging her in any way possible, that she should leave me.

I finally found the perfect home. And yes I was looking for a better place for the kids. But I was looking for something that had everything that she and I might want as well. A pool, a barn, a garage for a shop, a big yard, etc. And when I found it, I couldn't even get her to look at it with me. On three different occasions I asked her, and each time she said no.

One day she would text me about how she had no idea how I was ever going to be able to afford to buy that house. Then later that night she would text me and say the same thing, except she would add that she was proud of me for doing it. She was ll over the board. And It was becoming clear that these outside influences were beginning to ware her down.

On December 29th, 2016, after so many starts and stops, I finally closed on my house. And I told her I wanted her to be there. She wasn't, and she had no reason not to be. Just didn't. I spent the first 2 nights alone in my new home. Then the kids came home from their mothers. And eventually Louise came to see.

She never cared what my new home was. Never cared to be there. It never mattered that I bought it with her in mind. I don't believe she really ever even realized it. It didn't matter that I told her over and over. And it was never meant to be our forever home. Just someplace nicer for the kids in the meantime. And an asset to use for her and I when it was time for us to finally move forward together. That day never came. It was about 7 months later. She left me. I already told you the story.

When she finally had hit what appeared to be rock bottom, And realized she was drowning and needed to change some things, was the day she told me she wished she had not been so tuff all the time and just loved me through it all. At that point in her running stage I hadn't been contacting her. I wouldn't say I exactly surrendered. I was doing the work on my end to learn and grow. My energy was still flowing to her. I still prayed, probably 10 times a day for her, and her strength. And I still believed in us and one day she would find her way back to me.

She was drowning at the bottom of a pool, while everyone and all the people she surrounded herself with in effort to hide from us, just stood there and watched. That day I told her I would marry her, was me picking her up off the bottom of that pool and breathing life back into her. Something no one else could do.

From there it seemed we were on our way back towards reunion. But all pulling her off the bottom of that pool did was help her catch her breath so she could resume running. She had not dealt with any of her fears or grown in the time we were apart. She had however come to realize that the decisions she made were not what was best for her. Now in order to face her mistakes and put them right, she would have to face her fears as well. No matter how much she wanted to fix her mistakes, she couldn't get past her own fears. When Louise would start taking positive steps in our direction. That is, towards reuniting us, things would flow relatively smooth. Giving her the opportunity to face some of the mistakes and fears. But when it came time to do that, she caved. Every time. And every time she caved or went backwards, Life reached out and punched her in the mouth.

She had told me on several occasions that she was going to have a talk with the other man. On several occasions this never happened. And then the water damage to her house. She viewed this as a sign that she shouldn't leave. She should stay put. What she didn't see is it brought out the best in what could have been for us. And gave the opportunity for us to come together in something we both loved, and in a common goal. We had always loved to work together building things. And this would have been no different. I offered to move her to my home until the construction was complete. An offer that of course was refused. The more I begged her to let me help the more she hid. Going days without contacting me. And then, the universe smacked her again.

She and her business partner were now being sued, for copy write infringement. And it was no small lawsuit. Again, she went deeper into her hole. And again it was to her a sign that she needed to stay put. For me, I insisted she move with me, and she didn't even have to work if she didn't want to. She could just focus on the issues she was facing, and together we would be so much more powerful energetically, and able to accomplish more. Of course this was rejected as well. I tried to help financially, by buying some of the materials to get started while waiting on the insurance company. I would load the truck with insulation and drive it over and deliver it. And then want to stay and help install it. But she didn't let me stay. Id drop off the material and see her for a few minutes and id have to leave for some reason. I begged her to let me help. But she never would.

She began saying she was going to move back into the house while working on it, she never did. She was going to move over the business until it was done, that never happened either. Then she was going to move out of the other man's home and rent a place in town until the house was done. Nope, you guessed it, never happened. She did her best to assure me that she was going to make it happen. And each time it was a very exciting and happy development. But each time it never happened it was just sinking back to the bottom of that pool. But now I could feel myself being pulled down with her. I was losing faith in everything I believed, in her. Every time she would get my hopes up, she always had another excuse not to follow through. It was coming to the point that I didn't believe anything she told me. And I was right. As I write this today, she still hasn't left his house.

After all the excuses, life reached up and smacked her again. Now she was having health problems. Severe stomach and abdominal pain. She went to the doctor and was ordered to have biopsies done. She would tell me this, but no one else. And in the end, she had surgery to fix the issues. When this happened I again insisted she let me take care of her. To move back into her house and out of his, so I could be there to help her recover. Of course this request was denied as well. Yet when the surgery was complete, she told me that she had been scared that it might have been cancer. And if it had been, she would have just disappeared from my life because she didn't want me to have to go through it with her. But as soon as she found out it wasn't. She wanted to see me. Not him, ME . I really couldn't take much more of this. I questioned my sanity daily. Was I really just an obsessed ex-boyfriend that couldn't let go? Was there truly such a thing as a twin flame? Or was this really just a toxic relationship that I couldn't end. Serious questions I had to face, and pray over. The only answers that came were...Yes, I am sane. No I am not imagining things, and yes this was a toxic relationship whether it was a twin flame or not.

Louise never once asked me to go away. Never once said she loved the other man. She always told me I was the one she wanted. That she wanted us back. It was in fact her words that kept me hanging on. But it was her actions that spoke louder. All the while she's telling me she wants us, she was still going home to him. Something I couldn't get over. She was, in effect, making me be ok with the fact that she loved me, so it was somehow ok for her to be living in his house.

I begged her to let me help with the issues of the house being damaged, I bought materials for her without her even asking. And that's just the thing, she never would HAVE to ask. Where was this other guy? Didn't see him over there helping one bit. Didn't see him reaching for his wallet to help out the woman he claims to be in a relationship with. The woman that he asked to move in and live with him. Not one bit. I begged her to let me move her and take care of her when she was sick. I knew our energies together could heal us both. And I always took care of her when she was sick. But I didn't see him lifting a finger to help her. He would leave town for days on end for work and leave her to fend for herself. And maybe part of that is she didn't tell anyone, but there again, why is it me that she will tell.

Life just kept smacking her in the face over and over trying to get her attention. But she used the issues presented, as excuses to do nothing. All because she never dealt with any of her fears. She had no capability to overcome them. And she knew it.

When she finally read that book I gave her, it opened her eyes. The problem is, it seems to be too little too late.

AS of now she claims to be "Doing the work". She claims to have made a list of all her fears, and what to do to overcome them. But once again she succumbed to them and went backwards. I haven't been contacted at all in a week. I simply told her to prove it. It's nice that she may be awakening to the knowledge of what's happening. But it changes nothing for me. I've been lied to, spit on, insulted, cheated, everything you can think of. And not one of her words has been followed through on. So her telling me she's doing the work means nothing to me, until she proves it. She cannot be doing any real work on herself or us, while still living in another man's house allowing everyone including him to believe that they are this happy couple. So until she faces that fear of telling people the truth about us, and actually leaves him and his home, it's all Bull shit

Chapter 5

Ok, now I know that last chapter may have been a bit repetitive. But I wrote it to illustrate a couple points.

First, Louise and I were together for close to 4 years before the separation. But she began running and I began chasing, long before.

It is said that runners run because they fear the intensity of the connection. This fear is brought on by unresolved issues from the past. Or maybe a better way to say it is that due to her past relationships, and the heartaches and hurt she may have had to deal with, but didn't. She never faced those fears. Maybe never had to. Who knows, we are all different. But because of the intense love and connection, it brought fears to the surface. And because of those fears, its instinct for the runner to run and attempt to hide from them. But when you are brought together with your twin. No matter how hard you try, or how far you run, you cannot out run the connection. And the more you run the more the chaser chases you. The runner cannot face their fears, for various reasons. The chaser, usually a bit further into this understanding and a bit more enlightened, cannot give up on what he/she, recognizes as there twin flame.

Louise and I both recognized very early on that there was something extra special about this connection. To the point we would use the phrase, "God Given", on multiple occasions. But the deeper the feelings grew. The more scared of it she became. I can only assume that because of her past relationships, and the borderline mental and psychological abuse she had to endure, as well as fear for her own safety at times, she had trouble believing what she was in fact living and being given wasn't going to turn bad. So it became a sort of... do unto others ....only do it first, type scenario.

She wasn't just running, she was pushing me away very early on. And me as the chaser, I just kept coming. In my mind, I had to show her I wasn't like any other, and there wasn't anything to be fearful of. Every time she voiced a complaint about something I did or didn't do, I surely argued with her. I didn't believe she was valid in all her complaints, but in the end I fixed whatever it was anyway. And she would move on to find another. And so on.

She had even said on a few occasion, to just let her go. She wasn't the one for me. But then again, it wasn't just me holding on. It appeared that way, but she was no more going to let go of me than I was interested in letting go of her. But the fear and instinct to run was confusing. For both of us really. I knew at certain points I should just throw in the towel, there was no way I was ever going to satisfy her. But I couldn't. Literally couldn't. Like something or someone wouldn't let me give up. And she felt the same. She couldn't give up, but she damn sure wanted to. She wanted to be away from me chasing her. To her that would end the fear and she wouldn't have to deal with anything. Except she thought she would be losing me in the process.

With a runner, there is always an excuse to run. And as chasers we try to take that excuse away. And when we do, the runner just finds another one. It escalates to the point where the runner will say some of the meanest, downright despicable things to intentionally hurt the chaser. When that doesn't work, sometimes they will do the one thing they know you won't stand for. All in an attempt to make YOU leave THEM. This is common. But all it really does is tare the chaser apart in a way no one can understand unless you have been through it.

For me. I won't repeat the things she said to me to intentionally hurt me. But she did. And she knew exactly what buttons to push. And still I kept chasing. I could not and would not let go. And it finally came to the point where cheating was potentially involved. And it was too much to take. Her definition, my definition, cheating means a whole lot more than spreading your legs. But in doing this, all the runner is truly doing is looking to put a buffer in between the two twins. And that is exactly what my twin did to me. The timing of when that buffer came into play? Well only she knows the truth. But whatever happened or didn't happen, I should have stopped chasing long before. But neither of us realized what was happening with us.

I chased because as long as I did she was still in it. She never really left, and I thought if I stopped or gave up. It would all fall apart. In reality, nothing was ever going to have a chance to heal until I did surrender.

Now I am at the end of my rope. I have no more to give to her. And in fact question the validity of the entire twin flame theory. How can this not just be another toxic relationship between a man that is heartbroken and cannot let go. And a woman that wants her cake and eat it to. A man that will cling to any and all hope of reunion, and a woman that strings him along unmercifully. As you can see both the flame and the unhealthy relationship scenario fit quite well.

I have read and researched the suicide rate among twin flame relationships. And although it is a hard number to come up with, it seems to be high. I can understand this, because if in fact this twin flame theory is legit, it is not at all for the weak. The pain and suffering both flames have to endure is unspeakable. So why do it? Why would anyone ever want to meet there twin flame, and become enlightened, if all that awaits is a life of pain and misery? When the alternative is ignorance is bliss. Life was so much better before an individual became aware of all of this flame journey stuff.

Well. Regardless of your answer to that question, you can't "unknow" something. And what I do know is that life is never fair. What she now knows is that there is in fact a reason that she can't let go either. In all the fears she has, and all the lessons she has yet to learn. In all the running she has done and still will do, she never let go. Why is that?

In my reading of other Twin Flame books and accounts, it is clear that it is actually rare when Flames actually do reunite, and live that happily ever after life we seemed to be shown the glimpse of during the "Bubble love" phase. I think it is only attainable for the strongest of souls. Not everyone gets the chance to meet their twin flame. The fact that you meet at all is a testament to the age, and wisdom of your soul.

Chapter 6

So now after all the hell and misery I have just written about, and all the lies and mistreatment, and suffering inflicted, why would I still believe? The answer is simple. I'm told to.

When a flame, usually the chaser first, becomes aware of what's happening, their consciousness is opened a little. And the more you open, the more you become aware of other things. Like the energetic connection between you and your twin. And once that is realized, it grows to a almost telepathic state. A point where you know what the other is feeling, and thinking. You know when the other is happy, or sad. Or needs your energy to help. You know when the other is thinking of you. Not just, well maybe, no, you know. You can actually feel them.

Synchronicities, cannot be denied, but are usually only recognized in retrospect. All the things, big and small that had to come together at just the right moments to bring you and your twin together. Impossible to be just chance.

Your guides pushing you to the path you need to be on. And when you are too stubborn to allow yourself to be nudged by your guides, they smack you in the face to get your attention. And when that don't work they do it again. And again, until you get it right. That's their job. That's the agreement you made with them before you were born, and they will never ever fail you. But even knowing this, WE are in fact, only human.

Your guides are always there to help and are quite anxious to communicate. All you have to do is ask. For me its feathers. My guides know that I recognize feathers as a symbol of this twin flame situation. So I find them everywhere. Usually after I pray for hope, or help, or strength. And they know that if I find a certain color feather, I'm going to look up the meaning of it. In this way they communicate.

I also wake up every morning with words from a song on my mind. I mean, as soon as I open my eyes. The words are there. Songs that may be 20 yrs. old, or that I haven't heard in years. Bu the words are always answers to my questions of faith or what I'm to do. If these things happen to you pay attention to them. Chances are your guides are trying to steer you to the right path for your journey.

For Louise it was feathers also. Remember I told you that on the day she left me, she looked down and saw 2 feathers laying at her feet. She had never had any special connection to feather before. But she said she felt compelled to pick them up. They weren't a sign that she would recognize up to that point. But they were symbols that I would recognize. And when she showed me them and told me, I was floored. I showed her the feathers I kept that had been presented to me as well. She never knew I equated finding feathers to my spirit guides.

Also for Louise, it was pennies. When she was on the right path, when her heart was where it needed to be. And when her love was with me and us, she would find pennies in the oddest locations. Just a single penny. To me this was her guides giving her reassurance that she was in fact on the right path. Only now is she recognizing what the signs mean.

She told me once that every day she is surrounded by everything that point to me. Her work shop, and all the projects that she now sells, that were originated together. Her dog. The Chocolate lab she bought just weeks before the split. The dog she always said she would never have. Yet there he was. Almost an exact replica of my dog. She would see my name everywhere, signs, on line, in books. My last name would be on the storefront of some place she happened to be driving by. The wine we made together. The hourglasses she loved so much and I had bought for her. All these things every day. Coincidence? No it was not. It was the guides trying to tell her to face her fears. Do the work. And get back to where she belongs.

As for what happens now? For me I really don't know. In my research, it says that once I truly surrender, I should work on myself, and learn to love myself as I love her. This is confusing as hell for me. Let's think about this. If she is my twin flame, and twins are both half of the same soul. Then by me finding true forgiveness for her, and unconditional love for her, aren't I really showing that same love and forgiveness to myself? We are the same.

Ironically, Kate basically said the same thing a couple weeks ago. I need to work on being present in my own life. Again, I wasn't exactly sure I understood. But as I thought about it. That's exactly what I have been doing since I gave up. Since I surrendered so to speak. I find myself, getting up early on a weekend and cooking breakfast for the kids again. I find myself being more "present" at work and taking joy in it again. I've had a few friends that need my help. The type of help only me and my expertise could offer, and I jumped at the chance to help. Instead of just disappearing and not wanting to get involved for fear of missing a message or call from my twin. I realized I have neglected a lot of things in the past 2 years. My growth stopped when I really became the chaser.

I remember telling Kate, that I was fine. I would live without her. But that there was no joy in my life. No happiness. I felt as if all I had to look forward to was a lifetime of solitude. And she knew this. She knew that I equated Louise with my happiness, and joy. And she was right. And I have to find a way to be happy and allow myself to have that joy, without her. And when I do, I will be really ready to move forward and grow.

As for now, I wake up every day, still with strange song lyrics in my head. And I give thanks for one more day. I ask for guidance each morning. I pray that today is the day that happiness finds me. In whatever form the universe sees fit. As long as there is joy. I also pray for Louise. Her strength and courage and knowledge. And that the spark within her never gets extinguished by all the layers of fear and hiding. I do still pray for her return. But only if it's for real this time. And if it isn't, then I pray that I am strong enough to make it through whatever the next phase of my life is, without her.

I am ready for the next phase of life. I do not want to face it without my flame. But I have to focus on doing just that. In doing so, I stop chasing. And hopefully give her the breathing room she needs to stop running and learn all that should have been. And can be. Learn the lessons and build the strength to finally face all her fears.

As for Louise, I can only speculate. I really don't know where she is at in her own head and heart. I know what she claims to want. I know what she said she was doing to get it. But whether the work she says she is doing is real or not I have no clue. Is she still doing it or did she run from it again? I do not know. But if she did run, I expect life to punch her in the mouth again. And it won't be pleasant. It never is. If she is in fact taking action to face her fears, I wish her the best. I believe that she cannot do most of this alone. But the first few steps she must. If she does not I fear she will be in a never ending cycle of repeating the same issues until she gets it right.

In the meantime, losing me, and my energy, through my surrender will either wake her up to the fact that she has no more time and no more options in this life if she is going to be reunited with the other half of her soul. Or she will sink into the fear and realization of her mistakes that landed her on the bottom of that pool in the first place. She will also give up, and give in to what in her own words she described as "the life she has and the easy way" instead of "the challenge of the life she wants".

I love this woman more than life. It is impossible for me not to. For all the negative things I have detailed in this book, such as it is, there are so many more wonderful things I didn't add to it. It is a book about the Twin flame journey after all. And that journey is not a pleasant one. I do not blame her for the things she did to me. I know I did not document all the mistakes I have made on this journey. There are two sides to everything. I'm reminded of the famous theory, "For every action, there is an equal and opposite RE-action" I know I am to blame for many of the actions and reactions on her part.

What will it take from her, for me to choose to once more move forward together? The basic simple things.

I clearly will not participate any longer in the triangulation she has used to make herself feel secure and hide from her fears. In a nut shell, that means I will not move forward until she leave the other man. I will no longer reach and give her the comfort of knowing I'm here for her, while she's there with him

I have to know that all this means something to her. That it means something that I held on when no one in the world would have. It has to mean something to her, and she needs to show it.

I have given and shown what true unconditional love really is. And shown what true forgiveness is. And I continue to do this. But I know that for myself to move on with trust and complete dedication to us, I need honesty. I need to know the truth about certain things that have happened along the way. And I need her to be willing to sit down, and unburden us both with the truth. Knowing she is already forgiven, by unveiling the truth, nothing can later sneak up on us and sabotage any of our future efforts. As it is said, "The truth shall set you free"

Anything else, we will work out together. Until then, I search for happiness. And pray for her, and the other flame. The one that burns deep inside of her, for us.

As of the date of publish, nothing has changed for us. I continue to seek guidance from the wonderful Kate, who I've come to view as a friend, and the only person I can talk to openly about this journey. Good thing right? I am after all paying her to keep me sane.

To my knowledge my Twin is still living with her other man. And I expect this will not change anytime soon. It is too easy for her to just try to ride it out until her daughter is graduated and his house isn't needed anymore. It will then become more convenient, for her to take action. Or so she thinks. The problem is, sometimes the runner and the chaser change roles. And the longer she remains silent and gives no effort, the stronger I become in the fact that I am ok alone. The longer it takes her to deal with her issues so that a reunion is possible, the more likely I won't be here when she finally gets her shit strait. And that's when she has the option to chase or not. To fight for us, or walk away. And I have the choice to risk getting crushed again over and over, or just stay in my safe spot where she can touch me anymore. Yup, a complete role reversal. The challenges of doing the work and actually changing and taking action instead of just talking or thinking have kept her from facing her fears. And she has given me no reason to believe any of this will change. My belief is that she wanted to string me along until such a time as it would be easy for her to make a transition. It has been 2 year. There will be no easy time. And while I continue to make a conscious effort every day to surrender, and not give the energy to her, in hope that it frees her to do what's necessary, it's more likely that my worst fears are being realized. I stop, it all falls apart. How could it not with no effort on her side.

So for now I say good bye. And apologize if this wasn't the easiest read, hey, I told you I wasn't much of a writer. If in the future there are new developments, I will certainly entertain the thoughts of writing a follow up edition. Assuming this one doesn't tank with the readers.

Till then. Good luck. Don't get burned by the flame.

Thoughts

- I guess what, in a way it all boils down to is, that together, the twins can heal a lot easier because of the mutual energy shared between them. Everything is easier together, than apart.
- It take a lot of energy to face fears and obstacles. And so much more to continue to hide and run from them. Conversely, eventually both need to learn that it takes so much less energy to just accept the love your flame has for you, and to work together once you realize and accept what the two of you really are.
- No one can break down your walls for you. You have to do the work to take them down on your own. And faith is essential. Faith in your twin, and there love. If you don't have this, you will never remove the walls and give you and your twin the chance to come together.

- 10,000 hours. I don't know exactly how long it takes to conquer fears and unresolved issues before you can truly come in to union. But when the chaser gives up, or surrenders, it's time to move forward. Your mind set has to be that you are moving forward in this life alone. If it's not, you could find yourself waiting years and years and wasting your life away waiting for something that just may never happen. There is no guarantee of reunion. Or that the runner will ever face there fears and unresolved issues. Deciding to move on is a choice that will be made when you are strong enough to make it, not when you are so weak from being beaten down by your twin. And just because you made that choice, doesn't mean you don't love your twin. And from research, most often this is when the Runner stops running and can address what needs to be fixed. Most often it's only after the chaser stops and surrenders that the runner can begin their work. All is not lost just because you surrendered. It's time to fix you! The chaser. Chances are you've neglected a whole lot while chasing. And now it's time to get back to being "Present" in your own life.

- The lessons and growth you both will experience, only matter if the knowledge is actually applied to your own life. I believe it the movie *Spiderman,* that we heard the expression,
  "With great power comes great responsibility"
  We have a responsibility to ourselves as well as our flame.
- It is easy for some to mistake the actual "Twin Flame" relationship, with that of an unhealthy, toxic relationship. Twin Flame or not, if it's toxic then it's time to look for an exit. And do not be too proud to seek help from a counselor or therapist. But be mindful of who you seek. Make sure it's a licensed professional that has some understanding of the metaphysical world as well. I just got lucky finding Kate. Or maybe on second thought it wasn't luck at all, divine timing, and a little nudge from my guides.

- Thank you Kate. Without your understanding and Guidance, I never would have made it out of the Darkness

Made in the USA
Middletown, DE
23 January 2021